Ja___ ___ ___ ___ business journalist as well as a TV ___ ___ ___ ___ humorist. She writes for the *Mirror*, the *Independent on Sunday*, *Marie Claire*, *Prima* and *Essentials* and has a daily column in the *Express*. Jasmine is the author of *The Money Magpie* and appears regularly as a financial expert on *GMTV*, *This Morning*, *The Wright Stuff*, *BBC Breakfast*, *Working Lunch*, *Tonight* and all the news channels. She presents online for BBC Raw Money, helping with financial literacy and skills for everyday life. She is also a well-known event speaker, bringing a lively take on an often dull topic. Jasmine is the director of Moneymagpie.com – an interactive consumer website offering comprehensive financial advice, daily offers and plenty of freebies for its readers.

# Beat the Banks!

Take back control of your money and
secure your family's financial future

## JASMINE BIRTLES

**Vermilion**
**LONDON**

1 3 5 7 9 10 8 6 4 2

Published in 2010 by Vermilion, an imprint of Ebury Publishing

Ebury Publishing is a Random House Group company

The Random House Group Limited Reg. No. 954009

Addresses for companies within the Random House Group can be found at
www.rbooks.co.uk

A CIP catalogue record for this book is available from the British Library

**Mixed Sources**
Product group from well-managed
forests and other controlled sources
www.fsc.org   Cert no. TT-COC-2139
© 1996 Forest Stewardship Council

The Random House Group Limited supports The Forest Stewardship Council (FSC), the leading international forest certification organisation. All our titles that are printed on Greenpeace approved FSC certified paper carry the FSC logo. Our paper procurement policy can be found at
www.rbooks.co.uk/environment

Printed and bound in Great Britain by
CPI Cox & Wyman, Reading, RG1 8EX

ISBN 9780091929473

Quote on page 18 reproduced with kind permission of HarperCollins Publishers
(*The Intelligent Investor*, Benjamin Graham, 1949)

Copies are available at special rates for bulk orders. Contact the sales development team on 020 7840 8487 for more information.

To buy books by your favourite authors and register for offers, visit
www.rbooks.co.uk

# Contents

# Acknowledgements

Thanks firstly to those who helped with the main research for the book – in particular marketing guru and editorial consultant David Ryder. Big thanks for loads of research and writing help from Paul Prowse, Tira Shubart, Sam Downes, Jack Griffeth, Mione Brackenborough and Divya Guha.

I'm very grateful to my business manager Anthony Newell for loads of fun ideas and for giving me the discipline and the incentive to write the book. Thanks to the marvellous Moneymagpie team for keeping things going while I was writing and in particular to Jo Robinson for running things so smoothly. I had great help and advice from Julian Knight at the *Independent on Sunday*, Moneymagpie blogger Cliff D'Arcy and The Motley Fool's David Kuo.

Thanks to the Vermilion team including, of course, my editor Julia Kellaway, the PR and marketing departments and the design and sales teams. Big shout, as always, to my literary agent, Euan Thorneycroft, and my managing agent June Ford Crush and finally (and importantly) to Elsa and Roger Buckle who so kindly put me up in their lovely home during some of the writing process (Villabigiolicorfu.com). Thanks to all of you I managed to get through this project with my sanity intact – relatively speaking!

# How to Use This Book

Hello and welcome to the start of taking control of your money away from the banks and into your own hands. This is a reference book for anyone wanting to make money for themselves.

You don't necessarily need to read it all, though. Here's a guide to getting the most out of it, depending on your circumstances:

## Chapter 1: Basic Rules
Use this chapter to re-think *how* to think about money: what it is and what it means to you; how to use and not abuse it. This chapter is for everyone, from those in debt to those with cups overflowing. Use this chapter to get an understanding of the value of money and not have someone else take it from you. Everyone should read this one.

## Chapter 2: Order of Importance
Are you wondering where to start? You know you need to save and invest but you just don't know how to take the first step. This chapter will show you the best order to do everything so that you maximise your money and minimise the hassle. This is a useful chapter for everyone. Read it!

## Chapter 3: How to Save
No one should start investing until they have built up a good savings safety net. This chapter is for you if you're out of debt but you're struggling with saving and you would like to get help on how to do it the best way.

Chapters 4, 5, 6 and 7

These chapters give you the information you need to get started with your investment portfolio. They cover the four main 'asset classes' that any investor should consider – shares, pensions, bonds and property. Everyone should have a mix of investments and these chapters will help you decide how to divide up your money between the different products. It's worth reading them all through and then going back to different sections to find out more about products you're still not sure about.

Chapter 8: Taxation

Yes, I know it looks boring but, honestly, everyone should read at least half of this chapter. The more you know about how to avoid tax, the richer you will be.

Chapter 9: Odds and Ends

This is my 'outside the box' chapter – most relevant for those with some capital and looking at more diverse ways of investing, from art to gold. Once you've invested in two or more of the basic asset classes in Chapters 4–7, have a look at these ideas.

Chapter 10: Products to Avoid

Definitely give this chapter at least a quick read. In this age of lies, confusion and financial services playing on our innocence, this chapter is my plea to you not to believe in the silly products the banks want you to 'invest' in. You have been warned!

# Introduction

> **What they want you to do:** continue in a state of ignorance so that you can be sold any overpriced financial product they can make money from.
>
> **What you should do:** read and digest this book; make your own investment decisions and calmly invest regularly over time to create a rich future.

Welcome to the brave new world of beating the banks at their own game!

For far too long we've allowed ourselves to believe that our banks and building societies exist to serve us. We have believed that our bank managers think and act like Mr Mainwaring in *Dad's Army*, that they have our best interests at heart and that they give us genuine, honest advice.

No way! It hasn't been like that since the 1980s when Thatcher's government opened the doors for unbridled commerce in high-street banks and allowed the suits in the City to get into all types of trading. When I say 'all types', remember the American 'sub-prime mortgages' debacle and how people in the Midwest defaulting on their home loans somehow caused some of our biggest (and many smaller) banks either to fold or be bought or bailed out? Well, there's an example of this 'trading' for you!

Since the commercial 1980s banks and building societies have become nothing more than money shops. They run and operate with their eyes totally on profit margins under the guise of 'care, service and protection'. But really the only difference between them and second-hand car salesmen is that our bank 'managers' don't wear medallions (well, not at work anyway).

The problem is, we carried on treating the banks as though they still had the same values as they had in the 1940s. We still believed that Mr Mainwaring was running things, whereas he had already been made redundant and the boys in white socks were sitting in his seat.

What we all need to get our heads around is the fact that all of these institutions are in the business of making money. They exist to make a profit – THEY ARE NOT THE NHS. I can't tell you how many times I have reiterated this on TV and radio and in print. Even the trusted Post Office bank is backed by the commercial Bank of Ireland. That friendly and free financial adviser recommended to you by your estate agent doesn't charge you because he's raking in the cash through commissions on dodgy products he advises you to have – this type of financial adviser is less adviser than salesman.

These businesses exist to make money. In fact, in the case of PLCs (such as the major banks, for example), technically their only responsibility is to their shareholders who, in turn, only want them to make a profit. In making those profits you would think that they should be mindful of their customers too, but for the last 20 years or so, they haven't had to care much because we took the rubbish they sold us without complaint.

## How Northern Rock Rocked Our World

Remember the day back in August 2007 when queues of people lined up outside Northern Rock to take their money out? It was like that scene in *It's a Wonderful Life* when there's a rush on James Stewart's savings and loans operation.

Until that day in August 2007 most people comfortably thought that their money was safe in banks . . . safe as houses! Here was when the nation began to wonder if their money should be better stored under their mattress. Safe manufacturers sold more safes in 2008 than they had in the last 30 years. Never before had the nation really considered the small print when we opened an account. We worked, we put our money into the bank confirmed by a monthly slip of paper, we never saw it or considered it, and then suddenly BANG . . . like a shot in the head, all but the filthy rich realised they had no power at all.

For years we've been fleeced, conned and sold down the river. We just didn't realise it properly until the crash that started in 2007 hit us, and suddenly all that seemed stable and part of the fabric of society revealed itself as rotten at the core and built on lies and dodgy dealings – mostly against us, the consumers.

It's not just the banks, of course. Building societies, financial advisers (or rather, financial salespeople), investment houses, insurance companies, brokers . . . you name them, have had their snouts in the trough, profiting from our naive trustfulness and, frankly, ignorance. They have sold us overpriced and underperforming investments, expensive insurances that we don't even need and savings and current accounts that have cost us money rather than made it.

## The Time-Bomb is Ticking – We Have to Take Things into Our Own Hands

One of the reasons why we have believed in banks for so long is that as a nation we have kept believing that the state would look after us from cradle to the grave. And we saw the big high-street banks as somehow part of that state, even though we have never had a state-run high-street bank (apart from the Girobank which lasted from the late 1960s to 1989 when Alliance & Leicester bought it).

In the last 30 years the majority of state provisions have either been significantly reduced or taken away completely. The problem is, we haven't noticed – or haven't wanted to notice – and we have continued to live as if all our personal needs would be taken care of by the government.

Now we have to grow up, wake up and smell the overpriced coffee shop skinny mochaccino. We have to realise that the state will not, cannot, provide for us in the way that it promised back in the mid-twentieth century. It can't fund our retirements, beyond the most basic provisions; it can't provide free care homes for all those who will need them in the future; it has already stopped providing tertiary education for free; our healthcare system cannot cope with the increasing demand and no one can be guaranteed a job for life.

All this is happening just at the time when life expectancy has massively increased (which is a good thing) but we are putting proportionally less and less into our retirement funds (which is a bad thing). Still believing that the state will provide and anyway 'I might die tomorrow' (I've had that said to me a few times by debtors in their twenties), we are spending the money we should be putting away on meals out, nightclub sessions, the latest fashions and yet another holiday in Ibiza.

We're setting ourselves up for an impoverished old age. Right now the basic state pension pays just £95 a week. Pensioners are supposed to manage on that. Can you imagine what it's going to be like in 20, 30 or even 40 years' time when we have an even greater proportion of people over 70 in the population and fewer of working age to support them?

We have to take financial responsibility for ourselves and, particularly, for our future. This book will help you do that.

## How This Book Will Help

My aim is that you learn to do as I do: spend a bit of time reading up and researching the best kind of products to invest in; put money in these products on a fairly regular basis; keep an occasional eye on how they're doing, then go out and HAVE A LIFE.

Seriously, it doesn't have to take all of your time and thought. Nor does it have to take all of your money. You can still go out and enjoy yourself here and there. In fact, my view of money is that it is simply there to support the lifestyle that you want. Money is not something that should take up any more of your time and energy than it absolutely has to. When you do have to think of it, it should be as your servant, not your master. Money is not to be feared nor revered. It is a servant, a tool. With the right knowledge you can make it grow on its own with very little effort from you, other than being willing to sacrifice a few inessentials now for bigger essentials later on.

Marketing departments in banks, insurance companies, credit-card providers, investment funds and the like try to get us worked up about money – either playing on our fear of disease and poverty (insurance companies) or our excitement at the prospect of making easy money quickly (investment funds).

With this book you will learn to ignore their persuasive messages, and to take with a pinch of salt the over-excitement in TV programmes and newspapers about the latest investment trend. It will teach you to think for yourself and go your own way. It's the only way to follow.

What I really want to do with this book is give you back the power . . .

- *This book will give you the tools to save and invest for your profit, not for the banks' profit.*
- *It will also give you the confidence to invest for real growth and real wealth for your future (and your family's future) without spending any more time and effort on it than you need to.*
- *This book will help you think for yourself – not think with the crowd, because one sure way to lose money on investments is to follow the herd.*
- *It will help you empower yourself to spend and invest to give you the most profit and the least wastage by putting your money in cheap and effective products rather than overpriced, packaged 'investments' thought up by profit-hungry banks and institutions.*

- *It will also show you how to do your own research (it's really not that hard) so that you can tell when financial institutions are trying to sell you rubbish and when you're actually being offered something decent.*

Because we really need to take back the power now more than ever. I was in debt once. I owed £10,000 and paid it off in a year. It was the best thing I ever did because it forced me to learn how the system works and how easy it is to fall into the trap of over-spending and ignoring the mounting interest on bills. As soon as I had my 'light-bulb moment', when I realised just how much interest I was pouring into the bank's coffers, I changed my ways totally. I worked solidly (seven days a week sometimes) to earn extra, I sold anything I could find that I didn't need anymore and spent not a penny more than I had to. I learnt my way through hard graft. I have learnt the system that most of us fall into and here I will show you how to truly live a richer life.

Remember – this is a fight for your money! And I want you to be able to use this book as your armour to BEAT THE BANKS!

**What they want you to think:** that you should follow blindly whatever you're told and let the 'professionals' play with your money.

**What you should think:** that you can, and will, think for yourself and act for yourself, investing, with the help of this book, in a simple, easy and effective way to provide you with a good income when you need it.

# Chapter 1

# Basic Rules

We get so much financial information thrown at us from every direction now.

Each day we're being targeted by so many different financial and insurance companies that it's difficult to sift out the good advice from the sales nonsense. Everyone is trying to sell us something and the confusing messages we get from the media don't help.

We're being sold financial products in the supermarket, on the Internet, on the TV, on the radio, in newspapers, on buses and billboards . . . But we always thought we could trust the banks – until now. Since the financial crash that devastated 2008 and the instability and turbulence of 2009, we've realised that we can trust banks even less than the others!

In that case, why invest at all? Surely what we've learnt from all this financial uncertainty is that keeping our money in a box under the bed is the most secure way of saving! Why should we invest when we don't trust the people we're supposed to be entrusting our money to? But even in these difficult times there are basic principles that you can follow that will help you sort the wheat from the chaff and become a smart and savvy investor:

- *Save before you invest*
- *Spread your bets*
- *Think for yourself*
- *Be a contrarian*
- *Get information*
- *Let your head rule your heart*
- *Be regular*
- *Protect what you have*
- *Watch the tax*
- *Avoid wasting the money you have*
- *Change investments as your life changes*
- *Shop around*
- *Don't think about it too much*

Keep these rules in mind all the time. If you do you will find that gradually the mist will clear and you will be able to spot products to avoid. Also, you will start to invest intelligently and with confidence. After a while, you might even add a rule of your own!

You see, really investing well for your future isn't about picking the right products or putting your money in the markets at the right time or being 'clever, clever' and knowing the secrets that no one else knows. It's about the way you think. It's an attitude of mind – a strong, independent, confident and informed one.

That's why I've made this list of rules the first chapter. I recommend that you read this one and the next chapter thoroughly, even if you skim through all the rest. Get a grasp of the basic principles and the fundamental ways to think. Make these your guides, your questions to yourself. They will protect you and your family's futures.

These will enable you to make sensible decisions; to hold your ground when all around you are either frightened or overly enthusiastic about a particular sector (like property or tech companies or corporate bonds or whatever happens to be in fashion) and often to do what sometimes seems boring now in order to have a glamorous time later on.

So read, and reread, the rules then go further into the chapter and learn how to think – for yourself – so that you can outwit the City boys and the banks and your supercilious brother-in-law who thinks he knows how to make money but actually doesn't. Get the knowledge and you'll do better than the rest.

> **What they want you to do:** buy any financial product they're peddling that makes them loads of profit and, therefore, loses you money.
> **What you should do:** ignore all the sales stuff, read through this book and make up your own mind about what you want to invest in.

# The Rules

## SAVE BEFORE YOU INVEST

As you will see in Chapter 2, there's an order in which to do things if you're going to make the most of your money short term and long term. There is no point investing for the future if you haven't get enough 'liquid' cash saved up to dip into for short-term expenses. By 'liquid' I mean 'easy to turn into ready cash and get hold of'. And before you set up a savings account, you should make sure you're out of debt.

As I show in Chapter 3, you need to have enough money, that you could get your hands on at a moment's notice, to keep you and your family going for a few months if everything went pear-shaped, or even if it's just a case of needing to replace the boiler or the family car.

The important thing is that you should not have to cash in long-term investments in order to cope with present expenses. Long-term investments can go up and down in the short term and you might find yourself having to sell just when the market is low. Also, many good long-term investments take a long time to sell (such as property) and that can be too late for immediate needs.

## SPREAD YOUR BETS

The biggest and loudest message I want to put across to everyone who wants to invest for the long term is SPREAD YOUR BETS.

As you will see from all the chapters in this book, the message continues from start to finish: DON'T put all your eggs in one basket, DO mix your investments. In other words, diversify.

The main reason I say this is because nothing in investing is certain. No one has a crystal ball and no one can tell you what is going to happen in the future. Nothing, no investment, not even houses, is as safe as houses. You cannot rely on any one asset class to create a nice pot of money from which you can receive a decent income later on.

The best thing, always, is to spread your investments across at least three different asset classes – by 'asset classes' I mean different types of investments such as shares, property, bonds and the like.

> **What they want you to do**: invest in packaged-up, 'unit linked' products that apparently spread your investments for you but do it at a high cost.
> **What you should do**: pick different asset classes yourself that you want to put your money in and spread your money yourself.

## THINK FOR YOURSELF – DON'T JUST FOLLOW ADVISERS

The next most important point of this whole book is that if you're going to beat the banks and make some sensible money for yourself (as opposed to lining their pockets) you have to THINK FOR YOURSELF.

Of course, as you're reading this book (and you will be following it up by checking the online resources at Moneymagpie.com, Fool.co.uk, Investorschronicle.co.uk among others) you are already thinking for yourself, which puts you head and shoulders above the vast majority of the country.

Keep it going. Develop (if you haven't already) a healthily sceptical approach to all claims made by banks, investment managers, fund managers, financial advisers and even financial websites.

Some will be good – financial advisers that charge a fee for their advice are likely to be half decent at least. Financial planners can be very helpful if you get the right one (see page

316 in Appendix 2 for advice on how to choose a good one). Some funds (if you pick the right ones) make money and some websites can be a fantastic source of information and help in your quest to manage your investments well.

Generally, though, most will be just out for your money. It's easy to be swayed, so keep reminding yourself, particularly when faced with a new type of investment that sounds like big, easy money, that they're not on your side.

Remember, when it comes to investments, if it sounds too good to be true, it is. Never wrong, that one – never!

> **What they want you to do:** buy investments that make nice fat commissions for advisers and nice fat charges for the fund managers.
>
> **What you should do:** think for yourself, invest in cheap, simple products with low charges and very little packaging.

## BE A CONTRARIAN – DON'T FOLLOW THE HERD

Make your own decisions rather than following what everyone else around you is doing.

It's not just financial organisations that can persuade us to lose our money in bad investments. The media, friends and family, colleagues and people down the pub seem to have a strange compulsion to get us to throw our money away with them.

In the 1990s everyone said that anything with dot-com at the end of it was a surefire money maker – until the bubble burst in 2001 and many lost millions (literally). Then at the start of this century all the TV programmes and everyone's dinner party guest went on about how property was the only way to invest. Now, in some parts of the country, it will take years for houses to get back to the prices they were in 2007.

Remember, even top investors and businesspeople can be fooled if they let greed (particularly) and fear rule them. Don't be like them. Think for yourself and only invest if you think it's a good idea, not because your friends say it is.

Be different. Be a contrarian. Wear your pants on your head. Dress like it's 1979. Eat cake for breakfast if you feel like it. Sell property when everyone else is buying and buy shares when everyone else is selling.

As a great investor (and one of the richest men in the world) said, 'Be fearful when others are greedy and greedy when others are fearful.' It's possible that people are right to be fearful at a certain point (not often) so don't simply buy stuff while they're selling because it's cheap. Think about what it is that's being sold – it may not be worth the money even at that cut-down price. Don't be caught up in the excitement of possibly getting a bargain.

## GET INFORMATION

You really can manage your money and invest for your future as well as, and often better than, the professional investors, but first you need information.

Managing your money is like eating healthily. You don't need to be a qualified nutritionist to know how to eat well but you do need to know basic facts about fruit and vegetables, vitamins, protein, minerals, etc., to work out how to have a balanced and healthy diet (on that note, check out our healthy budget menus on Moneymagpie.com). Once you have that information it's up to you whether you use it (many don't) but you can't really carry on properly without at least a basic idea.

It's the same with managing your money. You simply need to get a good grasp of the principles of:

- *spending less than you earn*
- *saving regularly*
- *understanding compound interest (don't worry – it's very simple)*
- *investing in a range of simple, decent products*
- *keeping abreast of the main changes in the financial world (such as new tax-free investments like ISAs, good savings schemes, more generous rules on pensions, etc.)*

Then once you have this understanding you take action. Ditch your bad old habits – spending more than you earn, asking your bank for advice, not thinking about the future – to new habits that you learn from good, sound, financial information. It's as straightforward as that.

You can get more help and information by signing up to the Moneymagpie newsletter (which is free and sends information to your inbox every week) on the best ways to save, spend and invest. Go to the Moneymagpie.com homepage and sign up there.

If you would like more advice on investing, come to one of the Moneymagpie investing workshops. Just go to www.moneymagpie.com/workshops to find out when the next one is and how to enrol.

As you can change your eating habits to healthier ones, so you can change your spending and investing habits to ones that make and save you money instead of ones that just waste it.

> **What they want you to do:** stay ignorant and just be 'advised' by your bank salesman (usually called a manager) as to which of their rubbishy, expensive products you should invest in.
>
> **What you should do:** get some financial knowledge and keep it topped up every so often by reading relevant websites mentioned above and articles in the Money sections of weekend newspapers. Get some basic knowledge and make up your own mind.

## LET YOUR HEAD RULE YOUR HEART

Greed and fear are two of the most harmful emotions for investors. Boredom and laziness are also a problem. Be aware of all of these and get more discipline to fight them or they will steal your cash from you.

Be like the experts: stand back, do the calculations (get someone else to do them for you if you can't be bothered yourself), think things through for yourself rather than just reacting to what everyone else is saying and only buy if you really think it's worth it.

Always, always talk your plans through with a wise and trusted friend, or message me on Moneymagpie.com (even better, send me a question by video) and I'll give you as much help as I can.

In this book I'll cover various types of investments and, as I said above, it's important to invest in a good variety of different kinds of products. However, it's important to invest in the more solid, tried-and-tested asset classes first before going for fun, creative stuff.

For example, you need to be investing regularly in, say, a pension, stock-market ISAs and be paying off your mortgage before you should look to 'invest' in a house in Corfu or your friend's new cake shop or a ceramics collection. These things are attractive, pleasant and fun but as investments they're much riskier than other more traditional ones.

Let your head rule for the first few years and once you have a goodly sum in your main investment pot then you can start to play.

## BE REGULAR

As in bodily functions so in saving and investing: it's a good idea to be regular!

It's all about setting up and keeping up good habits. So easy to make, so easy to break, but remember, investing money these days is vital to the quality of your retirement. It may seem far, far away but pick up any paper on any day and you will find a sad story of a poor pensioner struggling to come up with the money for their basic needs. Even if you have only a small amount of money left over each month (or potentially left over if you were to stop spending it on fun stuff), in the long run it's much better to set up a standing order from your bank account into a savings account and then into a good long-term investment than to wait until you are earning big money. Even small amounts of money, over time, can amount to a decent pot over the years.

Also, by putting money in at regular intervals you benefit from what is called 'pound cost averaging' (I'll explain this in Chapter 4), which means you catch the ups and the downs of a volatile investment, and in the long run this smooths out to an average, decent return.

The whole idea of being regular is also part of the discipline of good money management. It does quite a lot of the work for you, particularly if you do it by standing order. After a while you will not even notice the money going out as your spending adjusts to the lower amount you have to use each month.

Even if your income is erratic (like mine) you can still set up some regular payments and then top up your investments every now and then when you get a pay cheque.

## PROTECT WHAT YOU HAVE

If you go to see a financial adviser you will notice that fairly early on they will talk about insurance and making sure you and your family are 'protected'. This is for good and bad reasons. Undoubtedly, it is important to make sure that your health needs are protected, your children's needs are catered for and that your possessions such as your home and (legally) your car are covered. It's a good principle and one you should consider before leaping into big money-making ideas.

However, insurance commissions made to the financial adviser are pretty impressive and the first lessons advisers (many of them are still salespeople, remember, not really advisers) learn is that they should sell 'protection' of any and every sort. I know, I've done those lessons.

The result is that most of us are under-insured in some areas and over-insured in others. Like everything else, you need to get some knowledge of the insurance market and think for yourself when it comes to protecting what you have. I'll give you guidance on this in Chapter 3.

> **What they want you to do:** buy so much insurance that you end up insuring your insurance, particularly when it comes to 'life' products which are mis-sold all too often. They also want you to be lazy enough to stick with the same provider each year.
>
> **What you should do:** consider seriously what possessions and income need protecting and shop around for the best insurance products for them. Also, set up your own 'self-insurance' scheme (as explained in Chapter 3) where you create enough savings to cover your expenses for three to six months.

## WATCH THE TAX

Tax is a necessary evil of a civilised society; a way in which we all contribute so that shared services can be maintained. It's also a way in which governments can fleece us in order to waste our hard-earned cash in their own special way.

Whichever way you view it, tax is still something that has to be paid. It just doesn't have to be overpaid. After all, why spend all that time and effort working for your pay and thinking through sensible investments just to lose a load of it in over-payment of taxes?

As you will see in Chapter 8, there are tax-free and tax-deferred investments that you should consider. ISAs, pensions,

National Savings & Investments products and certain specialist investment funds don't attract tax. That said, it's important to look at the total net profit first and not just go for something because it's tax free. Sometimes, even with the tax incentive, the rewards are still too low to deserve investment.

Still, as a basic rule, make sure you make full use of all tax savings where possible and don't pay any more than you have to.

## AVOID WASTING THE MONEY YOU HAVE

It sounds obvious but you'd be amazed at how much people waste when they start to make more money. Also, it's easy to get out of good spending habits and into bad ones at any stage of life, particularly if you go through rough times – and who doesn't?

So once a year or so it's worth checking on what you're spending and how much is going out each month just to make sure that you're not wasting money that could be invested to create even more later on.

Every three years or so, just to get a clearer idea of where the money's going, do a spending diary for a month. We explain in Moneymagpie.com how to do a spending diary and what the benefits are (just put 'spending diary' into the search box and you'll find the information).

You simply carry a notebook around with you and write down everything you spend every day for a month. At the end of that period (or even two weeks if that's all you can stand), you will see where you keep spending and what could be cut back. My manager, Anthony, recently changed to the 'Value' brand of his favourite breakfast cereal and it's saving him £3 a week. And he actually prefers it! So he's saving £156 a year on something he had never thought about before.

I will bang on about these small savings that grow to big wealth to my nearest and dearest until I'm blue in the face!

You might find that you're spending hundreds on buying rounds at the pub or that taxis are taking a third of your income each month. It's quite a shock to see how imprudent we can be much of the time!

**What they want you to do:** spend, spend, spend . . . on anything and everything!
**What you should do:** spend on what you love and what matters to you. Save on things that aren't important to you.

## CHANGE INVESTMENTS AS YOUR LIFE CHANGES

You could divide most types of investments into two main types:

- *Safe: pretty secure, rather dull, low risk and will bring you guaranteed but fairly low returns (e.g. savings accounts, gilts, investment-grade bonds, some pensions).*
- *Risky: potentially high return and volatile but, over the long term, they should make you very good money, but, then again, might not (e.g. shares, high-yield bonds, property, collections).*

Now, it depends on your general attitude to risk (you can do our online quiz at www.moneymapgie.com/bookgift to find out how adventurous you are as an investor) but as a rule of thumb, it's a good idea to use your age, roughly, as a guide to what percentage of your money you should put into these two types of investments.

So, for example, if you are 20 you should look to putting roughly 20% of your money into nice, safe investments (example 1) and 80% into the more volatile products in example 2. This is because you have a nice long time for the more volatile investments to go through all their ups and downs and for these movements to smooth out. If you're 40, though, you might like to put more of your money into the safer investments. However, if you are more adventurous and you reckon that you've got at least another 25 years for your investments to grow you might find the idea of switching to the duller investments too much to bear. In which case, ignore that rule of thumb and invest where you like. Go on – take a punt!

However, when it comes to about five years before you plan to retire it is a good idea to 'lifestyle' your investments and start moving your money from the more volatile, 'growth' products (shares, property, commodities, etc.) to the more stable invest-ments such as savings accounts, bonds and gilts so that you can capture the gains you have made over the years and keep it going even if you happen to retire just as markets are falling.

This, of course, is fine unless that five years happens to fall in a recession! If you are nervous about the economy it would be best to start 'lifestyling' earlier than just five years before you want to retire. You may lose out by taking your money out of stocks and shares, for example, but at the same time it could help you sleep easier. During the credit crunch when I was asked what people should do if they were about to retire, my answer very often was 'try and put it off for a year or two'. Increasingly we have to be more flexible about the time we retire as economic circumstances are more regularly volatile.

In Chapter 6 I cover income-bearing investments, i.e. places where you put your money and it keeps paying you a return month after month or year after year. These are the kind of investments you need if you want an income without actually working for it!

It used to be that these kinds of investments were only recommended to people who were over 50 – those who were either retiring or moving towards retirement and would be looking for, a) more stable investments to move their money to, and b) investments they could actually live off.

However, lifestyles have changed and, as Timothy Ferriss excellently demonstrates in his book *The 4-Hour Work Week*, many people are having time out early on in their lives between different work phases. People in their twenties, thirties and forties want to go round the world or just take time out to do something other than work. For these people, income-bearing investments can be good for the short term too. So you don't have to be over 50 (or more likely, now, over 60) to be thinking about 'lifestyling' your money.

Generally, though, most of the investments in this book are about growth because I have assumed that you have some time to go before you plan on hanging up your briefcase for good and getting into gardening.

> **What they want you to do:** stay with their products for the rest of your natural life whether it suits your needs or not. They just want you to keep paying their management fees.
>
> **What you should do:** as soon as a product isn't right for you, for whatever reason, ditch it and move to something else.

## SHOP AROUND

It's a fundamental principle of money management generally, and it's important in every type of investment, to shop around for the best deal.

This doesn't always mean the cheapest deal or the lowest charges but most of the time it does (as you will see later in the book, one of the major factors that affects the growth of your investment over time is the management fees charged).

This is where money websites, online fund supermarkets and, sometimes, independent advisers can be very helpful. They can lead you to the funds with the lowest charges, the mortgages with the lowest interest rates and the lowest-priced SIPPs, for example.

It's important to shop around in every area, particularly when you come to choose an annuity from your pension if and when you retire. Too many people simply take whatever their pension fund offers, not realising they can shop around in the whole market. As a consequence they lose out for the rest of their lives. Don't let that be you – there are always different or better options if you spare the time to look!

> **What they want you to do:** give absolute loyalty to your bank or any other financial company you have done business with. They want to sell you all the other products they have and get you to renew all policies and investments with them without looking for better value elsewhere.
>
> **What you should do:** shop around, shop around, shop around. Shop around, shop around, shop around. Shop around, shop around, shop around.

## DON'T THINK ABOUT IT TOO MUCH

Money is such a dull thing I sometimes wonder why I write and talk about it so much. It's probably because having no money is even more dull and I'm concerned that too many people know too little about money to help themselves. And once I was one of them – I really was! Realising the lies and misinformation I was given has put me on this mission to demystify money.

As I said above, it's as important to know the basics about money as it is to know the basics of healthy eating. It's not a good idea, though, to be obsessed with either money or food. Both will create their own problems.

Interestingly, being obsessed with money won't even make you more money. The people who are, in the long run, the most successful at making money are generally people who are not exclusively interested in money. As the economist John Kay puts it, 'There are many people in financial markets who, although not necessarily stupid, are characterised by extreme vulgarity of mind and expression.' Don't let that be you!

So take some time to think about what's important to you

in life and then go for it. Think about money only in so far as you need it to live in the way you would like to.

---

> Money is not to be feared or revered. It exists to help you do what you want to do in life and that's it. When making money becomes an end in itself you're lost, both morally and, often, financially.

---

Get information from this book, and elsewhere, about how to invest; invest your money regularly; keep a general eye on your investments say once or twice a year; then forget them and go and live. Otherwise what's the point?

# How to Think

Most people who come to my workshops and seminars on investing and managing your money have no idea how much money they're aiming to amass. In fact, they have no real idea of how much their actual net worth is right now let alone what it could be in years to come.

This is pretty normal for the UK. Most of us have had little or no financial education and it has come as a horrible realisation to us in the last few decades that our future wealth and security really is now our own responsibility. Successive governments will be able to do less and less to support us because they can't keep up the promises made in the last century.

As a nation, to a large extent we are still thinking and acting as though things are the same as in the last century when we could expect the state to provide education, health, pension and, often, a job for life. All of these certainties have gone. They really started to fall away in the 1980s but we are still taking our time grasping that fact.

## WHAT ARE YOU AIMING FOR?

So, take a big deep breath and think about what you really want from life, and what you're going to need to provide for yourself now that you really can't rely on the state.

What kind of life do you want to lead? Are you impulsive or cautious? Do you save then binge or do you binge then save? Do you plan holidays or book last minute when you're burnt out? All of these factors must inform your investment decisions and your financial reprogramming.

Financial planning has traditionally been about developing a nice pot of money to retire on in a few decades' time. That's still what most people aim for – if they aim for anything. But our lives have changed. We're not so rigid or traditional now. Many people take sabbaticals, decide to have a gap year in their forties, think about taking time out to have children or just have an easy time of it for a couple of months a year (if their work allows it).

This might be you too. But either way you need to sit down and consider what your medium-term and long-term plans are (in an ideal world) and work towards supporting those plans financially.

## HOW MUCH DO YOU NEED?

As with anything, when it comes to investing for your future it really helps to have a specific goal to aim for. The question is – how much?

Unhelpfully, the real answer is 'it depends on you'. In other words, it depends on what you want to do with the money, when you want to retire, or semi-retire, what your liabilities are now and what they might be in the future. Ultimately, everyone is different and everyone has different financial needs.

However, as a starting point, let's think about an average amount of money you might like to live on when you stop actually working for your money and start wanting simply to be given it . . . just for being you and being marvellous!

The national average wage at the time of writing is around £23,500 (about £25,000 for men and £22,000 for women – go figure). If you wanted to throw it all in today and have an income of around that figure just from your own investments, you would need to have amassed a pot of money of around £400,000.

This is because, in general, the kind of interest rate you can expect (averaged out over the years) for nice, stable, income-bearing investments is about 5%. So if you turned some of your £400,000 pot into an annuity (an investment that gives you guaranteed returns for the rest of your life) and/or long-term savings bonds or gilts or other stable, interest-producing invest-ments (see Chapter 5), you would be paid somewhere in the region of £20,000 a year plus or minus a few grand depending on the prevailing interest rates.

It doesn't end there though. That £400,000 figure assumes that you're retiring today, this year or thereabouts. If you're planning on retiring in 30 or 40 years you will need more than that to produce a higher income to compensate for the effect of inflation. And we're still just talking an income equivalent to the national average wage, remember!

Let's assume an average rate of inflation over the years to be 2.5% (because that is roughly what the Bank of England has been instructed to keep it at over the last 10 years). If you're planning to retire in 20 years you would need a pot of money of just over £650,000 just to keep up with inflation and not lose any value. If you're going to wait for 40 years then you will need over a million. Of course, inflation won't necessarily stick at 2.5%. The average rate of inflation over nine of the last ten years was 2.7%. Since December 2008 it has dropped to around 1.5%. It could go way above that in the next couple of years. This sudden change demonstrates that inflation is liable to alter at the drop of a hat, and one thing you can't count on is a fixed or entirely predictable financial market. Expecting such great stability could very well be your undoing. For a more extreme example look back to the 1970s, when inflation averaged out at 13% annually, peaking at 25% in 1975. These years have skewed average inflation figures for the last 50 years, which measures at 7%.

Always keep that in mind – check Moneymagpie.com regularly for our updates, trends, charts and advice. Inflation in the UK has the regularity of our weather!

> Inflation is essentially the amount that things go up in price each year. Each year the Office of National Statistics finds out the average prices of a 'basket' of goods – a collection of products and services that the average family buys in the year – and it works out how much those things in total have gone up or down in that year. If the prices have gone up then we have inflation. If the prices have gone down then we have deflation.

On the plus side, the longer you wait to retire the more time your money has to grow so don't be too appalled by these figures. Time is on your side thanks to the 'joy and wonder' of compound interest.

In fact, compound interest is so important a subject that I urge you to take a moment to read the following short and simple explanation if you don't already have a good grasp of the concept:

## COMPOUND INTEREST MADE EASY

When you invest money you earn interest on it (or you should do anyway). The following year you earn interest on both the money you originally put in and on the interest you made during the previous year. The next year the same happens and so on and so on. Each year your money grows by a greater amount.

For example, if you put £100 into something that gives you 10% return each year, at the end of the first year you will have made £10. If you keep that money in there then you will make 10% on £110, which is £11 – this is added to your total, meaning that you now have £121 earning interest. Then in the next year you will earn 10% on £121, which is £12.10. So you can see that each year it goes up just that bit more.

| Year | Capital | 10% interest | Total at end of year |
|------|---------|--------------|----------------------|
| 1 | £100 | £10.00 | £110.00 |
| 2 | £110 | £11.00 | £121.00 |
| 3 | £121 | £12.10 | £133.10 |
| 4 | £133.10 | £13.31 | £146.41 |
| 5 | £146.41 | £14.64 | £161.05 |

The two things you need to know about compound interest:

1.  Small differences in interest rates make a big difference in the long term.
2.  Saving regularly over long periods of time can build up a large sum of money. Look at the compounding box below. Imagine putting £100 a month into something giving you 10% a year for 40 years. Over 40 years your meek £100 a month would turn into a roaring £559,460.

| Year | Capital carried over | Capital added | Total capital | 10% interest | Total at end of year |
|------|---------------------|---------------|---------------|--------------|----------------------|
| 1 | £0.00 | £1,200 | £1,200.00 | £64.05 | £1,264.05 |
| 10 | £1,264.05 | £10,800 | £12,064.05 | £8,081.71 | £20,145.76 |
| 20 | £20,145.76 | £12,000 | £32,145.76 | £40,252.87 | £72,398.63 |
| 30 | £72,398.63 | £12,000 | £84,398.63 | £123,530.47 | £207,929.10 |
| 40 | £207,929.10 | £12,000 | £219,929.10 | £339,530.99 | £559,460.09 |

## HOW MUCH SHOULD I INVEST EACH MONTH?

How much you should save depends on your financial position now and what you're aiming at. But as a general rule of thumb, and something that doesn't take too much effort, take your age, halve it and use that figure as a percentage of your income that should be invested for your future. So if you're 26, about 13% of your income should be invested in various things for your future (that can include your pension, ISAs and so on). If you're 46 then 23% of your income should be invested. The figure goes up as you get older because you have less time for the money to grow.

That rule of thumb is only partially useful though. If you've invested nothing until you turn 40 then just putting 20% in each year isn't going to cut it. If possible you should put much more in to make up for the lost years, or simply decide to retire later. On the other hand, if you're suddenly making squillions in your forties then 20% may be enough to create the kind of pot you would be happy with in a few decades' time.

The other thing to calculate occasionally (really, only do it occasionally because these things happen very slowly so there's no point obsessing about it) is how your investments are growing and, roughly, how long it's going to take (and how much more money from you) to get the amount you're aiming for.

## THE RULE OF 72

One way to work out how long it will take for your investment to grow to the required size is to use what is called the 'Rule of 72'. This is where you divide 72 by the percentage rate of growth of your investment – don't panic, it's very simple.

If your investment gives you 8% a year on average, it will take nine years for your money to double (72 ÷ 8 = 9). It will only take six years if you're getting 12%, and so on.

If your investments are averaging about 10% a year and you have £50,000 now it will take another seven to eight years for that money on its own to turn into £100,000. If you'd like to build that pot up faster you need to put in extra over the next few years.

## HOW MUCH CAN I EXPECT TO MAKE?

Another thing to keep in mind is what kind of rate of return you should be aiming at, and expecting, each year.

Remember, for long-term investments you may find that some years you make one amount, say 5% return, and other years you make more or less or even lose on your investment. But if the investment is any good, over time those ups and downs should be smoothed out and the general direction of your investment will be upwards.

It's useful to have at least a ballpark figure of what you're aiming at, and what different investment vehicles (actual products you invest in) generally produce. That way you can tell if your investments are doing well or not.

What I do, and what I suggest you do, is to aim (or at least hope) for an annual gross average return of 10% (that's before tax and inflation). Let's assume that the tax on your earnings is going to take away about a fifth of that (leaving you a net return of 8%) and inflation (which is roughly 2–2.5% a year) will erode the value of the return further. So in real terms you will make a real return of 5-6% a year. (An exception to this is the investments you hold in ISAs and other tax-proof 'wrappers' which should make more.)

You can make even more by reinvesting dividends that you get from any shares or share funds that you own, i.e. using the annual returns to buy more shares or generally add to your investment portfolio. In fact, unless you desperately need the money in one year, I suggest that you simply make it an automatic thing that all dividends are reinvested.

Once you know that 10% is a good (actually slightly high but often achievable) return to expect, that puts other investments into context for you.

For example, the majority of people in the UK prefer putting money into savings accounts (either online or in high-street banks and building societies) to putting money into the stock market or pensions. Cash ISAs are far more popular than equities (shares) ISAs.

## WHAT IS AN ISA?

ISAs are tax-saving wrappers that you wrap around an investment to stop you having to pay tax on any gains. You can get cash ISAs and stocks and shares, also known as equities ISAs.

With a cash ISA, effectively you set up a savings account (with a building society or bank) but when you get your interest (usually monthly or yearly), the government won't take tax out of it. With shares ISAs, if your investment grows, you won't be taxed on that growth. We all have an ISA allowance each tax year (6 April one year to 5 April the next), which is essentially a limit on how much money you can contribute to your ISA.

ISAs were set up to encourage people to invest for the long term, which is why the government allows us to put the full allowance (currently £10,200) into a shares ISA, while you can only put £5,100 into a cash ISA (plus another £5,100 into a shares ISA, if you want). This is because the government knows that long term, shares offer us a much better chance of making money for our retirement than cash does.

It's up to you how you put money into your shares ISA. You can put in just a lump sum or a few lump sums, or you can make monthly investments. It depends on your circumstances what you do here. If you have a lump of money to invest now, then go ahead and put it in. But if you don't, and you think you can afford a certain amount each month, then set that up as a direct debit from your bank account.

While the average return of the stock market has been 10.1% since the launch of the FTSE All-Share index in 1962, the average return of cash investments (savings accounts) has been 5.7% in the same period.[1]

Nice, safe government bonds (gilts) generally return about 5%. The return on 'with-profits' life-insurance policies (the kind of things financial salespeople love to sell because they get big kick-backs for them) over the last 10 years has been 2.7%!

You see the difference? You see how important it is to:

- *Look at long-term average returns and not be swayed by returns over the last year or so?*
- *Not listen to financial salespeople who don't have your best interests at heart?*

# How to Spot a Dud Investment

Sadly, there's no fail-safe way to spot a loser otherwise there would be a lot more millionaires and billionaires in the world.

However, there are some pretty sound principles to keep in mind that will at least protect you from the very worst 'investments' and help you mitigate the effects of the not-so-good ones.

[1] Source: www.pru.co.uk/investments/guide/cash/

There are two types of dud investments:

- *Absolute rubbish that was bad from the start – possibly even fraudulent (there are always a few of those around).*
- *Investments that are perfectly good in principle but, for one reason or another, perform badly for a time.*

The answer to dealing with the second type – investments that don't do so well for a while – is to make sure you don't have all your eggs in that one basket.

As for the first type, there are definitely ways to spot some of them and protect yourself from others:

- *Always keep in mind that 'if it sounds too good to be true it probably is' when you read or hear of amazing, easy-money schemes that are 'guaranteed' to make you rich.*
- *The more the hype, the more you should worry. Big ads on radio, on the Internet or even through word-of-mouth usually mean a dodgy idea that you should avoid.*
- *Don't go to investment seminars that are run by individuals or companies with a vested interest. Property seminars run by development syndicates who want to get you to invest in their portfolios, investment seminars run by fund managers or people trying to get you to sign up for an expensive series of investment classes should be totally avoided. These are just sales events aimed to get you into a closed room so that they can brainwash you into handing over your cash.*
- *Ignore all 'tips' from friends down the pub, your brother-in-law's dodgy mate, someone your mum met at the hairdresser's or even your best friend who should know better. If you're really interested in what they are suggesting then do your own research, talk to people who genuinely know and then make up your mind.*

- *Anything that promises returns of more than 10% a year (particularly those that guarantee it) should be approached with extreme caution. They are highly likely to be bogus.*

- *Watch out for new investments connected to whatever is the fashionable asset class at the moment (by 'asset class' I mean 'thing to invest in', such as property or shares or commodities). For example, during the property boom all sorts of funds and seminars connected to residential and commercial buildings were peddled and far too many punters lost a whole lot of cash through them.*

- *Pretty much anything that your bank is trying to sell you should be regarded with the utmost suspicion. This goes for all financial products, not just investments. If your bank tries to get you in for a 'consultation' always say no unless, of course, you're severely in debt and have asked for their help in changing your repayments. It's simply a sales talk and if you are naive enough to go, be prepared to come out having had your pocket picked.*

- *Any schemes you find online where there's one long web page with big headlines blaring 'I made $30,000 in one week!' or similar. These are all bogus and laughable at best.*

- *Anything that is suggested to you over the phone by a cold-caller from a so-called investment company with a 'dead-cert' investment product. This is likely to be a boiler-room scam (see opposite) so if you get one of these calls just put the phone down, or, better still, tell them to wait a moment, put the receiver down on the table and go off to make yourself a cup of tea, wash the dishes, do the ironing, read a book, get married and do whatever else you like until the caller realises that he's been had.*

## THE 10% MAGIC TRICK!

The 10% figure that you've kept in mind in order to figure out the best product to invest in will also help you to spot scams and frauds. It is certainly possible to achieve much more than 10% a year with some investments – there have been a few (very few) investors and funds that have done a lot better than that – but nine times out of ten, anyone trying to sell you a product that they say will bring in 15% or more per year is a liar and a fraudster.

Properties in Northern Ireland rose sharply from 2004 to 2007, peaking at an annual growth rate of 51% before dropping like a stone once the credit crunch hit, falling by more than 28% in 2008. It was during the bubble that various companies sprung up offering investors the chance to build million-pound property portfolios just by investing thousands in their seminars and then in their own property scams.

Other people have been taken in by Ponzi schemes offering eye-watering annual returns and no apparent catch. The catch is that Ponzi schemes (named after Charles Ponzi who ran the first such operation in 1920) work by getting more and more investors to put money in and simply using the money of new investors to pay off the old ones. This works well at first until it inevitably gets harder to find the new investors and the whole thing unravels, often leaving the newer investors losing thousands.

There are also what are called 'boiler-room' scams. In fact, a fun way to find out about how these work is to watch the film *Boiler Room*. What you learn in the film is that boiler rooms are dodgy stockbrokers who create artificial demand in the stock (that's American for shares) of defunct companies by cold-calling investors and selling them shares at stupidly high rates. Once the firm has finished pumping the stock the investors have no one to sell their shares to and the price plummets. The investors lose everything. Really experienced, sophisticated investors get duped by these scams so if they do then new investors are even more likely to be taken in. If you get any calls or emails telling you there are fabulous riches to be had from putting your money into this or that company, just say no and run a mile.

So keeping the 10% mark in mind and keeping a check on your greed levels, you should be protected from the most smooth-talking of 'investment' salespeople.

So, now you have the basic rules for investing and managing your money in one go. Take a break, put your feet up, have a cup of tea and digest what you have read. These are the rules that you should live by when considering your investments.

## Chapter 2

# Order of Importance

'**F**or everything there is a season' and that's as true for investing as it is for life generally. Long term you will make more money with less effort if you do it in at least roughly the right order. Trust in financial institutions is at an all-time low so there couldn't be a better season than now to take stock of your current situation before you ask yourself:

## Where Do You Want to Be?

What are you aiming for and when? There's no point investing if you don't have goals – things to invest for, things you want to do and things you want for your family. Ten is a good number to aim for on each list – one for yourself, one list for you and your partner, one list for your family. You don't have to stop at 10 but it's a good number to get you going.

Write down all the things you'd like to do with your life, the places you'd like to see, the experiences you'd like to have. What would you like to provide for your family? What are your education goals for them, their future needs and the things you'd like to do as a family? Let your imagination roam around, don't stint yourself, put down what you'd like in an ideal world.

Go crazy – is it going to see Niagara Falls? The Grand Canyon? Perhaps you want a pilot's qualification? Really, this here is your life. Come up with ideas to give you financial responsibility and, most importantly, inspiration.

Nothing is set in stone. Personally I'm not good at planning things. I like spontaneity, being surprised by life and going in new directions that I had never even thought of. There's nothing wrong in that and there's no reason to plan things to the last detail and force yourself to keep to it.

All plans should be flexible and they can be updated and altered as circumstances change. But it's useful at least to have an idea, a few reminders, of what you would like to be able to do now and in the future so that you can have a decent idea of why you need to save and invest. It doesn't half concentrate the financial part of your mind!

For inspiration visit My50.com where you can see other people's lists of 50 things to do or have.

Speaking of not waiting to do them, remember, as I mentioned in the last chapter, that you don't have to set aside happy experiences for retirement only. More and more people are taking gap years and sabbaticals during rather than just after their working lives. This can be you if you plan it right. Keep that very much in mind.

# Where Are You Now?

The second stage in preparing yourself for future investments is to determine your current financial position. You need to know where you are in order to know what you have to do to get where you want to be. So, off-putting though it may sound, before you make any investment decisions you need to work out your current net financial worth, where you are in your life and what you want to do with the rest of it and what your attitude to risk really is (as opposed to what you might think it is).

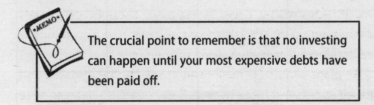

The crucial point to remember is that no investing can happen until your most expensive debts have been paid off.

## HOW MUCH ARE YOU WORTH?

Get a pen and paper (back of an envelope will do) and write down a list of your financial assets – property, shares, savings, car, saleable goods, trust funds, etc. – and then a list of your liabilities – mortgage, credit-card debts, overdraft, hire purchase, money owed to family, etc. If you are married or in a civil partnership then do it with your spouse because your legal status as being part of a couple affects some of your financial issues.

Take away your total liabilities from your total assets and that will show your net financial worth. Here is an example:

# NET WORTH CALCULATOR

|  |  | Liabilities | Assets |
|---|---|---|---|
|  |  |  |  |
| Cash | Current accounts (negative if overdrawn) | -£160.00 |  |
|  | Savings accounts |  | £2,500.00 |
|  | Other cash holdings |  | £300.00 |
|  | Bank loans | -£5,000.00 |  |
|  | Credit cards (total including store cards, Visa, MasterCard, etc.) | -£8,500.00 |  |
|  |  |  |  |
| Home | House (current market value minus 10% to allow for costs of sale) |  | £155,000.00 |
|  | Outstanding mortgage | -£130,000.00 |  |
|  | (net value of the home is therefore £25,000) |  |  |
|  |  |  |  |
| Personal | Car (immediate sales value minus 5% to be safe) |  | £1,800.00 |
|  | Outstanding total car loan | -£800.00 |  |

# ORDER OF IMPORTANCE

| | | Liabilities | Assets |
|---|---|---|---|
| Personal | Collectables (art, stamps, bonzo dogs, etc., at conservative valuations) | | £150.00 |
| | Jewellery (saleable items that you would be happy to sell) | | £0.00 |
| | Student loans | £0.00 | |
| | Other | | £0.00 |
| | | | |
| Investments | ISA(s) | | £3,000.00 |
| | Mutual funds | | £0.00 |
| | Stocks and shares (current value – 15% to be safe) | | £0.00 |
| | Bonds | | £0.00 |
| | Other | | £0.00 |
| | | | |
| Retirement | Pension (current value) | | £120,000.00 |
| | Pension (costs of releasing now) | -£40,000.00 | |
| | | | |
| Other | Any other assets | | £0.00 |
| | Any other liabilities | £0.00 | |
| | | | |
| Totals | | -£184,460.00 | £282,750.00 |
| | | | |
| Net worth | | | £98,290.00 |

The amount you have outside of the net value of your home is the most important figure. If you have started to accumulate funds then that will give you a good basis from which to take the next steps in this chapter.

In the example above the bank loans and credit cards (-£13,500) are greater than the investments (£5,800). The person has the ability to clear their debts immediately only if they sell their house and/or cash in their pension. If neither of these is an option then they will need to cut expenditure and, if possible, increase their income to pay off the shortfall.

If your net worth is negative then you're in a difficult situation and all your focus needs to be on getting out of the red, at least in terms of your credit card debts and other general loans and overdrafts. The mortgage is a lower priority because the interest you are paying on it is probably lower, it will be harder to pay it all back quickly and you need somewhere to live! That said, you will save thousands of pounds if you pay your mortgage off as soon as possible as I explain on page 56.

To find out more about getting out of debt and developing the all-important cash cushion go to Moneymagpie.com and/or take advantage of the clever tricks and money-making strategies in my previous book, *The Money Magpie* (also by Vermilion). If you would like to ask me questions directly and hear from other finance professionals, come to one of our Moneymagpie Money Management workshops. Just go to www.moneymapgie.com /workshops to find out when the next one is happening and how to enrol.

# What's Your Position?

Next you need to take a good hard look at yourself. Your investment, and other financial decisions, are affected by your age, your income(s), what financial responsibilities you have – such as children to bring up or other dependent relatives – and what time frame you would like to set yourself for achieving your various financial goals.

> If you haven't already created a budget for yourself you must. You can get a free downloadable budget planner at www.moneymagpie.com/bookgift

It's a good idea to get down on paper some facts about your situation, your family and dependants, your assets and liabilities and what you are hoping to achieve in financial terms. It provides a useful jumping-off point for your investment plans as well as a good dose of reality about your current situation.

To give you a head start, overleaf is a list of questions you should ask yourself. Either fill in the gaps here or copy out the list and add a few questions of your own:

Age and date of birth:_____

Marital status (including civil partnership):_____

State of health:_____

Children/dependants (list their names, ages, relationship and
state of health):_____

_____

_____

Other immediate family who might have a financial impact
on you now or in the future:_____

_____

_____

Your occupation:_____

Employer ('self' if self-employed):_____

Basic salary (estimate if self-employed):_____

Overtime/bonus/commissions:_____

Benefits in kind (specify):_____

Alimony (coming in):_____

Benefits and tax credits received regularly:_____

Life cover?_____

Pensions?_____

Other financial investments (e.g. ISAs, savings accounts,
shares, buy-to-let property) – specify and give value of
them:_____

_____

_____

_____

Family home – value, remaining mortgage:_____

Are you concerned about protecting your income?_____

What age would you like to retire?_____

How much would you like to live on when you retire?_____

What plans do you have for your children's education?_____

_____

Are there any major changes you want to make in your life in the next few years? What?_____

_____

_____

# What is Your Investor Personality?

The next step is to decide what your attitude to risk is.

It's important for you to know what you're comfortable with, in terms of where you put your money and what would keep you awake at night, so you know what kinds of investments to avoid.

Are you a gambler looking to make the big bucks or are you super-cautious and terrified of losing a penny? Most people think of themselves as being somewhere in the middle, wanting to make a steady income but not really willing to lose much along the way.

But even the ones who have a 'medium' attitude to risk have varying approaches to different situations and types of investments. Many also find that their attitude changes as they get older. Be honest with yourself. The only judge of this inventory is you. You have nothing to lose, and may even gain, by being blunt about your personality type.

# Get in Order

Lay the foundations or your financial house will collapse. I've set out the steps you need to follow in order to build a solid house that will protect you and yours for years to come. Ignore these steps at your peril!

## PAY OFF DEBT – THE DEVIL'S IN THE DEBT. IT JUST KEEPS ROLLING UNTIL YOU TAKE CONTROL

Debt is the devil when it comes to making money for yourself. It's probably the single biggest barrier to wealth for most individuals.

Before you even start saving, any non-mortgage debt needs to be paid off and paid off as fast as possible.

Credit-card debt, overdrafts and loans, particularly secured ones, need to be paid off as a matter of urgency. Look at Moneymagpie.com's 'Debt Issues' section for advice on how to pay off debt quickly and cheaply, how to 'snowball' your debts and how to get free help if you need it.

The only exceptions to this are cheap debt such as student loans and credit card debt at 0%. However, even these debts should be nagging at you until they are eradicated.

Those credit cards that offer 0% are fast disappearing from the market, which makes it harder to switch outstanding balances at the end of the 0% period. They all now charge a substantial fee (usually about 2.5–3.5%) to switch each time, which will add to your costs. So even these debts should be paid off as fast as is practical. Also, although student loans are cheap, while you still have some to pay off it can make it harder for you to get a mortgage.

## BAD DEBT VS GOOD DEBT – WHICH IS WHICH?

Bad debt is the expensive sort, the credit-card debt and loans that are taken out for unnecessary general spending (holidays, clothes, entertainment) that doesn't get paid back immediately.

Good debt is cheap borrowing in order to invest in a home (mortgage) or in your career (a student loan). This type of borrowing I would encourage but once out of the more expensive debt no intelligent investor should be wasting money paying interest to banks and credit-card companies for silly spending.

Having established that mortgages constitute good debt, they are still debts that need to be paid off and, as you will see on page 56, I consider that paying off your mortgage quickly and early is a particularly safe and profitable form of investment.

Keep an eye on the interest rate you're being charged for any debt you have and, if you can, switch to cheaper deals as they come along. Read the small print. Keep the ability to be in control if your situation changes. This is your handbook to beating the system, not getting sucked in deeper and deeper into the misery of credit-card debts followed by consolidation loans after re-mortgaging after a payday loan etc., etc. Remember, the devil is in the debt, holding you back, dragging you down.

## SET UP A CASH CUSHION

Once you have paid off the urgent and expensive debts the next stage is to set up cash savings for yourself. I go into this in much more detail in Chapter 3.

The aim of this next step is to create a pot (or a few pots) of cash that you can dip into easily if you need to. It enables you to pay sudden bills or keep things going during hard times without having to resort to selling assets you've invested in for the long term, possibly just at the time when these assets are suffering a dip in their value. Money you put into long-term investments should be left there for the long term.

The first thing you must do is save enough money, in a high-interest but easy-access (remember: these pay less interest) account, to cover your living expenses for three to six months.

By living expenses I mean everything from your mortgage and utility bills to travel, food and all the costs associated with running yourself and your family. So once again, if you haven't already done a basic budget (a list of your monthly incomings and outgoings) then do it now. That will show you how much you need each month to keep the roof over your heads and body and soul together. The free form can be found at www.moneymagpie.com/bookgift.

The idea behind the three- to six-month period is that generally it takes around that amount of time for people to recover financially (and often emotionally) from problems such as redundancy, divorce or other life events that stop them earning money for a time. Without a cash cushion, just a few months of little or no income (even with benefits coming in) can tip someone into serious financial difficulties.

Once you have collected enough money for this cash cushion then you can start investing. But it's also useful to continue with other short-term savings for major purchases such as a car or a new boiler and also to create liquid (i.e. easily accessible) funds for yourself so that you can take advantage of new, very good investments when they appear.

## PROTECT WHAT YOU HAVE BUT DON'T BE FOOLED

The insurance industry is large and lucrative and much of its income comes from exploiting the fear and ignorance of UK consumers. Here is where you have to be extremely careful. Use this book. Use your head. Use Moneymagpie.com – it's at your disposal! You can get all kinds of weird and wonderful insurances including pluvius insurance (insuring against rain ruining your event), multiple birth insurance (yes, really, you can get insurance against having twins or triplets) and particularly cynical disease insurances such as specific cancer insurance which was quite obviously dreamt up by the marketing department of particular insurance companies playing on the big fear so many people have. And we can all be scared. It's so easy to be when you see the recent crisis on all financial levels. Keep calm and follow this advice.

When thinking about which, if any, insurances to take out, do it in this order:

- *The insurance you are legally obliged to have – basically motor insurance. If you have a motor vehicle you have to insure it, end of story. Just make sure that you shop around (probably on the Internet is best) each year to get the best rate. Try the comparison services on Moneymagpie.com, also Kwikfitinsurance.com, Comparethemarket.com and Confused.com.*
- *Buildings insurance, if you have a mortgage, is usually a requirement of the mortgage company. Strictly speaking, it's*

*optional, but the lender may insist you have this cover. If the property were to collapse, the lender would want to know that there is insurance to cover such a catastrophe. For this reason, most people are sold building insurance when they take out a home loan. Again, shop around on the Internet for this. Don't just accept the one offered by your mortgage company.*

- *Insurance to protect your family. As soon as you have children you should take out life insurance on the lives of both parents. It doesn't have to cost too much: see the article on Moneymagpie.com for more details. If you are employed, check first to see if your employer includes protection in your salary package already. If so, you don't need to get your own!*
- *Lifestyle insurances that help you sleep at night. Home contents policies should be taken out by anyone who has more than just a few possessions – including students who often have more than they realise. If you travel regularly then take out a well-priced annual travel policy (as always see the comparison facilities at Moneymagpie.com). Specific items of value such as gadgets, jewellery, musical instruments and bicycles should be insured separately if they're not covered by your home contents policy.*

Think twice before diving into income protection insurance. It isn't what it sounds. It won't insure you against redundancy – nothing much does other than offensively high-priced policies with caveats in each line. It may cover you against loss of earnings through long-term illness that prevent you from earning for several years. Whether or not you should go for it really depends how afraid you are of this happening.

Private medical insurance (PMI) – as tiresome as PMS and an even more complex animal. It's increasingly expensive as medical procedures rocket in price and many policyholders come across too many exclusions and exemptions just when they need the money most. However, with the increasing likelihood of reductions in state benefits and NHS coverage, there is more and more reason for individuals to take out PMI.

With something as complex and expensive as PMI, I recommend that you use a good insurance broker who can talk you through the kinds of policies that would be right for your own personal circumstances. Comparison services aren't enough help. This is one of those products that demands one-to-one consultations. Good brokers that specialise in PMI include:

- *The Private Health Partnership – 01274 588862*
- *Healthcare Partners – 0800 066 5604*

When it comes to protecting your income, and giving yourself peace of mind, really the best policy is your own self-insuring cash cushion as explained above. If you create a good savings pot for yourself and your family, you will remove the need for many expensive commercial insurance policies and have the advantage of creating a growing pile of cash if you haven't needed to dip into it.

---

**What they want you to do:** insurance companies, and many financial 'agents', are desperate to sell you all kinds of policies that supposedly protect your income.

**What you should do:** set up your own 'cash cushion' that will cover you if you lose your source of income for a while. If you don't need to call on it then you will just have some extra cash to have fun with!

## CONSIDER PAYING OFF YOUR MORTGAGE

I'll say it loud and I'll say it proud like I'm on a megaphone, on a float at a radical political march, in fact I'm shouting . . . PAY OFF YOUR MORTGAGE AS FAST AS POSSIBLE.

Take note: financial advisers are not taught to tell people to pay off their mortgage. They are, however, taught to push insurance products and insurance-based investments. Co-incidentally, financial advisers make no money from you paying off your mortgage or existing debt, but they DO stand to make commissions from recommending insurance products and investments. Funny that.

I love the idea of paying off your mortgage early (I paid mine off in nine years) because:

- *It gives you the most wonderful freedom (particularly if, like me, you are self-employed and have to create work each month to make the payments!)*
- *It is tax freeeeeeee – any money you overpay into your mortgage saves you the full amount of interest, unlike savings accounts that will tax you on the interest you pay.*
- *It is one of the safest investments you make – when you pay off your mortgage, you pay it off and that's it. There is no uncertainty about what will happen to your money.*
- *Once it's paid you own your home outright – no longer does it belong to the bank manager.*
- *The mortgage companies hate it because they lose money! And don't we just love the upper hand?!*

To pay off your mortgage as quickly as possible you will probably need a flexible type of home loan to do it. If you currently have a fixed mortgage the chances are you can only overpay about 10% a year. Depending on how long you have remaining on the fixed deal and how much the lender would charge you to switch out of it early, it may be worth staying with the fixed loan until the end of its term and then switching to a more flexible product. While you're with the fixed loan you could pay off the 10% (or whatever the maximum is) and also set aside money in a savings account to pay off a lump of the mortgage as soon as you come out of the fixed term.

Remember that the more bells and whistles you get with a mortgage (this includes extra flexibility) the pricier it is likely to be. Fixed-rate and capped deals tend to be cheaper than others because they don't offer much flexibility and give the lender the security of knowing they've got you for at least the next few years.

If you have only just bought your home and are finding it quite enough effort to pay the mortgage each month then don't even think about switching from your cheap, fixed deal. However, if you have extra cash, have cleared your debts and are well on the way to amassing enough savings to keep you going for a few months then now would be a good time to go for a more flexible mortgage that allows you to overpay at any time without penalties.

In fact, if you really do have a good sum in savings and you plan on building up more then it would be worth looking at offset and current account mortgages. The two work in very similar ways.

With an offset mortgage your home loan is lumped in together with your current account and savings accounts so that any money you have on the plus side – the money that comes into your current account and the money that sits in your savings 'pots' – is offset against your mortgage.

This means that if you have borrowed £100,000 including your mortgage but you have combined savings and current account money of £20,000 you are only charged interest on £80,000. You still pay the same amount into your mortgage each month but more of that monthly payment goes into paying off the capital (i.e. the amount you owe not the interest you are being charged on it) because you are being charged less interest.

It does mean that your savings won't grow because they don't attract interest payments. However, you are better off overall because the money in a normal savings account would have to be taxed whereas using that money to reduce your mortgage is money that cannot be taxed.

The offset is a particularly useful mortgage for couples that are both working as you can both have your salaries paid into the account and start saving on interest from the moment the money hits the account.

Current account mortgages work in the same way except that rather than having a mortgage and various savings pots and current accounts it is all in one big current account which is constantly, massively overdrawn until you pay the whole lot off.

If you're interested in current account and offset mortgages you can get more information on them in Moneymagpie.com (just put 'offset mortgages' into the search bar). Also, download the Moneymagpie free mortgage guide at www.moneymagpie.com/bookgift.

> **What they want you to do:** mortgage companies really want you to keep your mortgage going for the full 25 years so that they make the maximum profit on the interest you pay. In 2009 mortgage companies grossed well over £60 billion on interest payments alone.
>
> **What you should do:** pay off your mortgage in less than 25 years – how much less depends on your circumstances. Also make sure you shop around when you come to the end of a fixed period so that you can get the lowest interest rate available, but make sure you factor in any fees your current provider charges to leave them.

## SET UP INVESTMENTS FOR GROWTH

Investing your money in well-performing products for the long term is probably the most fun aspect of managing your cash (yes, that did say 'fun'), simply because your money makes money for you while you sleep. That's my idea of a good way to earn.

Investing for the long term means investing for growth. You're not looking to get money out now but to keep putting money into something that will grow steadily over the years. Because we're thinking long term it's important to be bold in your investments and genuinely go for growth. So many people in this country can only bear to put their spare money into Post Office savings accounts, premium bonds and building society savings schemes that they will never benefit from wealth created without some research or similar effort. If you're looking to invest over a few decades then going for the 'safe' option usually means the option with the lowest return.

Far too many financial advisers, advertising agencies and financial company marketing people play on the uncertainty and fear they know is rife among the majority of UK consumers. They offer investments with the words 'guaranteed' and 'growth' and 'security' in their titles. They tell you that these products 'smooth out' the ups and downs of the stock market and that they are spreading your investment for you across 'different asset classes' perhaps by 'unit-linking' them. You can find out more about these kinds of products (and why they should generally be avoided) in Chapter 10.

Be bold and take your investments into your own hands. Ignore the fear and the hype. Read in this book how to invest in cheap, simple products that may seem scary in the short term, but long term are probably the most likely to create the real growth you need.

## HAVE A MIX OF INVESTMENTS

As explained in the previous chapter, one of the most important aspects of investing for yourself is to spread your bets. This means putting your money in a variety of investments including shares, pensions, property, securities (bonds and gilts), cash and all sorts of other possibilities.

It's not clever to invest in things you don't understand so do make sure you develop enough knowledge in at least three types of investment. The reason is that if one or more collapses (nothing is 100% safe) you have the others to fall back on.

The mix of investments you have will depend on your age, your attitude to risk and what is generally happening in the markets (although I do mean generally – there is no point trying to react to every up and down of the different markets as that's a sure-fire way to lose money and go mad!)

## MOVE TO SAFER, INCOME-BEARING INVESTMENTS

Although the majority of this book is about investing for growth (I have assumed a minimum of 10 years' investment time), it's also important to know how to make the most of those investments once you get to the stage where you want to live off them.

About five years before you want to live off your investments you should start 'lifestyling' them. In other words, gradually move your money from growth products to more stable, less exciting ones (cash deposits, bonds, gilts, for example). That way you are more likely to lock in the gains you've made over the years. If the market's in a downturn at that stage then the best bet, if you are able, is to put off your full retirement time for a year or two. Put off converting your high-growth investments for as long as possible until the market picks up and you can take a decent amount out.

It's crucial at this point to shop around for the best income-bearing products (i.e. highest interest paying) to make the most of the cash you have accumulated. Finding the right annuity is particularly important as that is supposed to last for the rest of your life. Annuities are what you buy with your pot of money when you retire. The amount you get from an annuity is fixed until you shuffle off this mortal coil so it's important to get the most you can possibly negotiate at the start.

There are loads of products to choose from. So, assuming you have paid off your non-mortgage debt, move on to the next chapter to find out the best ways to use the money available to you for saving or investing.

## HERE'S WHERE I GET REALLY EXCITED!

Now, let's move on to the first stage of investing for wealth on your own terms and beating the banks. Let's find out how to save and create the cash cushion that will stop you having to pay out to expensive insurance companies.

## Chapter 3

# How to Save

**O**nce you have paid off all your non-mortgage debt (apart from 0% credit cards and student loan money), the next step is to start accumulating money in a savings account or two.

## The Difference Between Saving and Investing

It's important to know the difference between saving and investing as the two need to be approached in quite different ways.

Saving is short term. It's about collecting up money to deal with things you want to buy – or things you might have to pay for – within the next five years. You need to have different types of savings (as explained below) but it's all the same basic principle.

You need savings for general emergencies and times when you might not be able to earn; savings for Christmas, holidays and a new car; savings for a deposit on a house; and general savings that just sit around in an account waiting for you to find a really great investment that you should put your money into.

You should expect to make money from your savings but not that much. The important thing with your savings is that they are safe and relatively easy to access. You want to know that if you put £100 in your savings this year you could go back to your account next year and find at least £100 still there. You should also know that you can get the money out with no more than a month's notice, if not instantly, should you need it.

Because you are going for safety primarily with savings you will have to sacrifice some of the money you could make on them. In other words, because you need to put your savings money into low-risk products with easy access (i.e. savings accounts) your reward will be lower. This is why savings accounts are good for the short term but bad for the long term because they don't give you enough money back to keep up with inflation.

Investing is long term. It's about putting your money away for five, ten, fifteen and more years in order to make even more money for yourself. It's money that you don't need for day-to-day spending. Money you can forget about until much later.

Money that you invest should be put in investment 'vehicles' (not cars, investment products like pensions, shares, etc.). These are investments that will make good money for you over the long term, even though they might go wildly up and down in the short term.

Money you invest is not money you should need to get your hands on in a hurry. The problem with trying to get hold of money you've invested at short notice is that you might take it out just at the time when that particular investment is at a low point. You could find that the £100 you put in last year is now only worth £95 although this time next year it might be worth £140. What's more, there could well be punitive charges for taking your investment out ahead of time.

This is why you need to save before you invest. You need to have cash at your fingertips so that if you suddenly need it to replace the boiler in the middle of winter or to pay for a fab holiday next month, you can. The money you take out won't affect your long-term wealth and you will have access to enough money to pay for what you need.

## Saving Fundamentals

Here are a few basics to keep in mind to maximise your savings.

Be regular – set reminders and work to small, pleasing goals! As I said in Chapter 2, putting regular amounts into savings (and investments) is much more helpful in the long run than putting in lumps of money here and there. This is mainly because it's human nature to find more interesting things to do with your money at any point in time than squirrel it away in a savings account.

However, if you set up a regular standing order from your bank account into your savings account and/or earmark certain earnings (maybe everything you make from a Saturday job or something similar) specifically for your savings account(s) then gradually, and almost without your noticing it, the money will accumulate.

Don't dip into your savings unless you have to. The problem with 'easy-access' savings is just that – you can access them easily. This is good if you have an emergency but bad if you're not disciplined.

If you think you will be too tempted to grab the cash for a big night out then go for one of those sneaky savings accounts that penalise you for taking money out (they usually cut out all the interest you would have made in the month that you withdraw) because that will put you off. Either that or go for an account with which you have to give 60 or 90 days' advance warning before making a withdrawal or else you lose the interest for that period. This should have the same disciplinary effect. A friend of mine keeps her savings details and cards with a sensible friend of hers and the deal is that she has to present a case any time she wants to dip in. Guess what – four out of five times she doesn't have one!

Have different pots – you don't have to do this but some people find it helpful to have different savings pots (sometimes in different banks and building societies) for different things. It helps them budget and work out how much more they need to save for specific things or events – it can also help when travelling abroad, i.e. some banks will charge more for overseas cash withdrawals.

It's also useful if you're in the happy position of having more than £50,000 to put into savings accounts as £50,000 is the maximum that is covered by the Financial Services Compensation Scheme if the bank goes bust.

It's a good idea to spread your money across different financial institutions too so that no one bank thinks it owns you!

Save in order of importance – as you will see below, the most important thing to save for is your personal insurance scheme, that is, your savings safety net. After that it's up to you what you think is most important for you and your family.

Have some liquid cash on hand for possible investments – one of the uses of cash savings is that it's liquid, i.e. you can get your hands on it quickly and easily.

That means that it's also useful if you hear of a good deal you would like to invest in now. Perhaps you have been watching a particular FTSE 100 company that you like and you see that their shares have suddenly plunged to what your detailed research tells you is less than their true value. This is the moment when it's very helpful to have easy access to a nice wad of cash that you can immediately use to buy undervalued shares. However, this is money that you should have over and above your safety net savings and your savings for other things such as a house deposit and holiday and Christmas savings.

**What they want you to do:** keep dipping in to your savings so that you have to use your credit card and loans to buy things you really need.

**What you should do:** work at maintaining your savings discipline. Make sure you always have a surplus. Spend time saving for things rather than insisting on having them now. As the saying goes: 'The bird of paradise alights only on the hand that does not grasp.'

# Most Important Savings Pot – Self-Insurance

This is money you save up to cover you and your family if you lose your job and can't work for a few months and there would otherwise be no money coming in.

First you work out how much you need to keep the roof over your head and keep body and soul together each month. Add up all your essential outgoings. This will give you the amount you have to have each month to keep everything going.

Once you have that figure, multiply it by three to six times as this is the number of months you would generally need to cover if you lost your job or something else happened to stop you earning.

For example, if you work out that you spend £1,000 a month on your mortgage, bills, food, travel, etc., then you should aim to have £3,000–£6,000 in your safety-net savings account.

Once you've saved this amount in a savings account, don't touch it unless you really are in an emergency. Forget about this money because it's your own personal insurance and you should just keep it there to fall back on.

> **What they want you to do:** take out insurances to cover yourself. These cost you and you will get nothing back unless you have to claim. Even then you may get a nasty shock when closer examination of the small print reveals that they don't pay you as much or as soon as you were led to believe.
>
> **What you should do:** insure yourself and your family as soon as you are able. If you can, and if it would help you to sleep at night, then put away enough to cover you and yours for a year.

NB This doesn't replace life insurance.

If you have children or other dependants you should take out a well-priced life-insurance policy. Shop around on the Internet to find the best policy for your needs.

# Other Savings

I've mentioned that it's a good idea to have different savings 'pots' for different things but there are also other ways to save.

## OFFSET MORTGAGES

If you have a mortgage, consider switching to an offset mortgage. An offset mortgage tends to have savings pots as part of the set-up. This allows you to get the best combined value between your mortgage payments and your savings earnings.

Briefly, offset mortgages work by lumping together all your current and savings accounts with your mortgage and any other borrowing so that the amount you have on the plus side is offset against the amount you have borrowed.

So (as I also explain in Chapter 8 on taxation) if you have borrowed £100,000 for your mortgage but you have a total of £20,000 in your current account and savings accounts, you will only be charged interest on £80,000 of your mortgage. You will still make the same monthly mortgage repayments but more of that money will go into paying off the capital of your loan rather than paying the interest.

This is a very simple example but it gives you an idea of the possible savings you might be able to make.

---

### WITHOUT AN OFFSET MORTGAGE:

Savings £20,000 at 3% interest after tax – earns you £600 a year.

Mortgage of £100,000 at 6% interest – costs you £6,000 a year.

Net position: £600–£6,000 = -£5,400 loss, i.e. interest charges.

---

## WITH AN OFFSET MORTGAGE:

Mortgage of £100,000 minus savings of £20,000 leaves £80,000.
£80,000 net debt at 6% interest costs you £4,800.
Net position: -£4,800 loss, i.e. interest charges.

I've had an offset mortgage myself and found it a tax-efficient and money-saving way of running my finances. It also helped me to pay off the mortgage early. Being self-employed meant that it also gave me some useful flexibility.

However, it's not right for everyone. Newer offset mortgages are often much more expensive than fixed-rate ones and for some people they offer too much flexibility and can mean that they never pay off their mortgage. You see, once you've paid off some of your mortgage you're allowed to borrow that money back again later. So if you've paid off £10,000, you could take that amount out again and spend it. If you're naughty you could find that you're constantly paying some of the mortgage off and then borrowing it back again so that you never actually pay the whole thing off!

## SAVINGS BONDS OR FIXED-RATE SAVINGS ACCOUNTS

Another type of saving to consider is what are called 'savings bonds' or 'fixed-rate savings accounts'. These perform a slightly different function from easy-access accounts.

In return for promising to keep your money in the account for a fixed amount of time, usually six months to five years, the bank promises to pay you a fixed rate of interest for the entire time (that's the 'bond' element of it – you both promise each other to keep your respective halves of the bargain).

The advantage of these accounts, particularly in a time of falling interest rates, is that you know what return you're going to get and generally it's a better one than you would get with an easy-access account.

However, the disadvantage is that you can't get your hands on the money if you need it before the end of the 'bond period'. What's more, if interest rates go up you will lose out relative to what you could have made elsewhere.

These are best for those who want real stability for their money or for those who want a fixed 100% predictable income from their cash. They tend to be beloved of older people, particularly those close to or at retirement age. This pre-dictability means that during tough times savings bonds can be a good haven for your money, at least until economic conditions improve.

During the credit crunch when interest rates, property and the stock market were falling like a stone, cash accounts, particularly short-term savings bonds (one- or two-year ones) were hugely popular with people desperate to put their money somewhere where they wouldn't see it reduce in value before their eyes.


## SHOULD YOU BOTHER WITH A CASH ISA?

In general my answer is 'no'.

My view of ISAs is that they are best used for long-term investments. Cash is the epitome of a short-term 'investment'.

I see ISAs as part of my retirement fund and therefore I put the full amount I am allowed each tax year into shares-based investments like tracker funds (see page 99) or ETFs (see page 104) or even corporate bonds (see page 177). To me, therefore, putting some of my ISA allowance into a cash-based one is a waste as, over time, cash accounts (savings accounts) do not perform as well as other asset classes.

However, if you are still worried about investing in securities (shares, bonds and the like) then you might as well save tax on your savings accounts by putting money in a cash ISA – it's better than nothing. Also, if you are close to retirement then it's probably a sensible idea to go for a nice safe cash ISA where you know what income you will get.

If you're retired and you can claim back the tax deducted from your interest, you may not want to bother with a cash ISA as its chief advantage is you don't pay tax on any interest.

The other catch with cash ISAs is that the highest rate will only be applicable to savers who deposit the whole annual allowance as a lump sum. And a high number of cash ISA rates include a 'loyalty' bonus, as the rate of interest includes a bonus – usually 0.5% – that is paid only if no withdrawals are made during the first 12 months. If you have to take money out, the rate drops.

## Alternative Ways to Save

Here are a few other types of savings accounts – some of them are so different they could be 'asset classes' in their own right. Once you have set up at least one basic savings account for yourself, consider some of these options.

# CREDIT UNIONS (CUs)

Credit Unions are basically not-for-profit financial cooperatives that offer a low-interest and easy-to-use saving and borrowing method for their members.

They have historically been particularly good for people on low incomes who want to save or borrow small amounts. But many Credit Unions are getting bigger and they now offer a range of services including current accounts, Christmas savings, mortgages, savings accounts, children's accounts, cash ISAs and fixed-term savings. So if you're a saver, rates of return can be higher than those offered by the main banks. At the very least it's worth seeking out your local one (you'll find it through Abcul.org, the website of the Association for British Credit Unions).

Credit unions aim to pay a dividend on savings once a year to all their members. This can be as much as 8% of the amount that people have saved, but is typically 2–3%.

Another extra bonus offered by Credit Union savings accounts is that life insurance is included at no cost to the member, making it easy to build up a useful nest egg for you and your family. On a member's death, the amount of savings can be as much as doubled by the insurance and paid to whomever the member chooses. It's also pleasant to know that City fat cats (and some of those cats really are fat! Whisky drenched and eating rich!) aren't pocketing profits on your transactions.

There aren't many Credit Unions in Britain, mainly because of restrictive financial rules in the past, and they're not very well known generally. However they are big in America, Ireland, France, Poland and several other countries around the world.

The way they work is that they are set up and run by a group of individuals who have something in common. For example, they may live in the same borough or do the same job (nurses' credit union, cab drivers' credit union).

Credit Unions charge a nominal one-off opening fee, often as little as £2. However anyone wishing to open a current account must join the Credit Union and open a savings account first.

## ZOPA.COM

I know, it's an odd name; it sounds like a Mediterranean soup. However, it is really a different form of savings account. In fact, if you put your money into Zopa.com you are called a 'Zopa lender', not a saver, for the simple reason that you actually are lending your money to other people that Zopa has carefully selected.

When you put your money into a bank or building society savings account your money is then used by the financial institution to lend to other people. You don't know who your money is lent to and you don't really care because as far as you are concerned your interest comes from the bank and is guaranteed by the bank.

The point of Zopa.com, though, is that your money is lent more transparently to other individuals. In fact, you even get the names (or usernames at least) and sometimes photos of the people your money is lent to.

You can find out what they will use your money for, roughly where they live and how old they are. Happily you don't lend all your money to one person. In fact your money is spread around quite thinly. No one borrower borrows more than £20 from any one lender. Many lenders (including me) cap their lending at £10 per borrower (although you can risk lending more if you like). This means that if one of the borrowers defaults then you've only lost a small amount of your investment.

Zopa makes money by charging lenders and borrowers a fee. Borrowers pay a small percentage (normally 0.5%) of their loan and lenders a 0.5% annual service fee. The interesting thing as a lender is that you get to choose what level of risk you are prepared to take and, therefore, the corresponding interest rate you will earn. This means that you can potentially earn a lot more than you would in the normal savings accounts. However, if you pick a high interest rate you may find that your money takes a while to be lent out as other lenders offering a lower rate of interest are grabbed first by potential borrowers.

You also need to decide how long you want to lend for (how many months your money will be tied up). You can lend for anything from one year to five years (another pay-off for the high-interest rates offered by Zopa is that your money is tied up for some time as with a savings bond). Often you make more money if you are willing to lend for more years.

Then you need to decide what kind of borrower you want to lend to. You have a choice between A-types (the top, most stable, high credit-score borrowers), B (slightly less impressive), C or Young (for borrowers aged 20–25). It certainly helps you realise what banks go through when they work out interest rates for their savers and borrowers!

There is a limit of £25,000 that you as an ordinary individual can put into Zopa. To go beyond that limit you need to pay £330 for a Consumer Credit Licence.

Zopa is a properly regulated financial institution (backed by US venture capitalists) so everyone who wants to borrow has to have their credit rating checked and they have to have been on the electoral roll in the UK for at least six years.

Zopa does have a strict credit-checking system but it has a rather more creative approach than some banks. For example, it might even take someone's eBay rating into account if they don't have many other things to show for themselves.

Although this is an alternative to investing with the banks, it's not necessarily a safe haven. One or more of the people who borrow some of your money (as the loan is spread around various savers) could default, although few have so far.

Putting your money into Zopa.com should be something you only do after you have enough money in a traditional savings account or two. It's also only for the more adventurous saver/investor who likes the idea of lending directly to other individuals and circumventing the banks.

Guess what – I'm a Zopa lender and I love the fact that I lend pretty much directly to other people like me.

> **What they want you to do:** stick with the high-street, retail banks that you know, giving them the benefit of your hard-earned money.
>
> **What you should do:** keep looking for alternatives and ways to make money without their 'help'.

## PREMIUM BONDS

I hate gambling in all its forms (I can think of far more interesting ways of wasting money than gambling with it . . . it's just like old ladies in Vegas, pulling levers and chewing gum to me!) but if you love to have a flutter here and there then a pretty safe way of doing it is to go for government-backed premium bonds.

Premium bonds are a scheme where, instead of receiving interest payments, savers have the chance to win cash prizes. The minimum purchase is £100 (or £50 if you pay by monthly standing order) and you can hold up to £30,000 of them at any one time.

The average return is around the same as (or a little less than) you would get from a normal building society savings account, even taking into account the fact that returns are tax free, but you don't lose your money as you do with normal gambling. Of course there's always the possibility that you could win the big one too, and also the possibility you might win absolutely nothing – ever.

Many people love them because they're excited at the possibility that they could win 'the big one'. If you're like this then by all means put some cash in, but not too much. Really, on average you would be better off putting more money in a high-interest savings account instead. Still, it's up to you.

## MONEY-MARKET ACCOUNTS

A money-market account is a type of savings account that earns interest just like any other savings account. The difference is that the interest rates you get are connected to the London Interbank Offered Rate (LIBOR) and not the Bank of England base rate, which is what normal savings accounts mostly track. The LIBOR rate is the daily rate at which banks borrow from one another in the money market.

Putting your money into these accounts is rather like playing with the big boys. You could make good money but you might make very little. They often call themselves corporate accounts, but they are also available to individuals who have a good lump of cash to put in.

You will need a big initial deposit even to think of saving in one of these accounts. Sums vary from bank to bank, but you will need upwards of £25,000 that you are happy to stow away just to get started. If you don't have anything like that in your piggy bank right now then move on to the next section (unless you're interested for the future perhaps?).

As the LIBOR rate is the price at which banks are prepared to lend to each other at any given time it is governed by market principles – i.e. it's about supply and demand, and rates are set according to what people are willing to lend for and what others are willing to borrow for (a bit like Zopa above). This means that the rate can be a lot more volatile than normal bank savings rates as the Bank of England base rate is set by a committee of learnt people who want stability, not volatility, in the economy.

However, many money-market accounts are fixed-rate ones, so you could fix a particularly good rate for a few years if you wanted. If you're not sure you can also fix a rate for just seven days. There are other accounts that are much more flexible and allow you to take your money out (almost) when you want although, as with bank flexible accounts, you will have to ride the ups and downs of the interest rates with those.

The vast sums needed to open most of these accounts mean that they only cater for a select few, and often better rates can be found with your more normal savings accounts, particularly in the short term.

Advantages of money-market accounts:

- *Most money-market accounts are immediately responsive to changes in interest rates, meaning if rates increase, you will benefit immediately. During the credit crunch when LIBOR was at an historic high, anyone with a money-market account would have been rubbing their hands.*
- *They offer flexibility to suit you – the account's term can be fixed from a day up to five years.*
- *The return you get from money-market rates will generally be higher than deposit-account rates offered by the same bank.*
- *They are conveniently managed – you can make changes to the account or close it over the phone.*
- *It's another way of diversifying your savings. If you're in the happy position of having a lot more than £50,000 to put into cash then once you've put as much as you want into normal savings accounts, money-market accounts follow a different interest rate and therefore might give you a better rate when normal savings returns are low.*

As with everything, though, there are also disadvantages:

- *Although it is likely that the base rate is only going to increase in the current climate, no one can be sure that the same will happen with LIBOR. In fact it could go down as the economy recovers and lending becomes more liquid.*
- *Commissions charged by banks on money-market accounts vary significantly – meaning different banks will offer different rates. You really have to shop around.*

- *Having said that, it's becoming increasingly more difficult to find daily rates on the Internet, making it more difficult to compare money-market rates from different banks and find the best account for you.*
- *Interest rates offered by money-market accounts are often more unattractive than those offered by other accounts such as fixed-term bonds.*
- *The minimum deposit for money-market accounts is typically around £25,000 – so many are not available to small-time investors.*

Although rates on money-market accounts fluctuate with wholesale money-market rates, some banks, like HSBC and First Direct, offer interest rates to be fixed for the term. First Direct also offer a money-market account with a deposit of just £2,000, opening the door for small-time investors.

Other banks to offer money-market accounts are RBS and NatWest, which ask for no minimum deposit and allow you to access your funds immediately and at no cost. But these things change all the time . . . so keep sharp and savvy!

So, are money-market accounts a good investment? It's difficult to give a straight answer on this, as accounts vary from bank to bank. Some allow withdrawals, others don't; some offer a fixed rate while others rise and fall.

Investing in a money-market account may suit you if you know you'll need access to your funds and you are able to invest in a bank that allows withdrawals. They are also ideal if you want a really short-term investment of as little as a week, or anything up to six months.

But as long-term investments and general savings, there

are better options available. You can generally earn better returns on fixed-rate bonds than money-market accounts. Of course, investing in bonds does mean that you will be locking your money away for a fixed term and you won't be allowed withdrawals. But if it's a decent return you're after and you're comfortable with locking your money away, bonds are a better option.

## OFFSHORE SAVINGS

Investing in offshore accounts used to be the preserve of the rich and those who could afford clever and slightly dodgy accountants. Now, though, thanks to the Internet and the increased globalisation of our lives, ordinary people without posh accountants and brokers are becoming interested in tasty-looking, potentially tax-free returns in other countries. International banks offer easy-access accounts, notice accounts, bonds and regular savers with interest rates of up to 5%.

Anyone can qualify to open an offshore account but don't imagine that you will save tax by investing in such savings or bank accounts. If you are a resident in the UK and it's your long-term home you will still be taxed, as although you receive your interest gross from these accounts, you have to declare it as part of your income on your self-assessment return (see my note about it on page 231). HMRC is tightening up on all offshore investments every year and seeking out tax avoiders and evaders. Beware, chaps!

Savings accounts vary from bank to bank and country to country, but in order to receive the best rates, you may need an initial deposit of £5,000, £10,000 or even £25,000. Some accounts even ask that you maintain a minimum amount in your account – as much as £3,000 – otherwise you may receive a decreased interest rate, while others only let you make a certain number of penalty-free withdrawals.

Generally speaking, as in all financial products, the higher the rates, the higher the risk. Institutions outside the UK (now including Irish banks) are not covered by the Financial Services Compensation Scheme (FSCS) – the protection scheme that guarantees up to £50,000 of your money in any one account should your bank or building society go bust. Sometimes they will have their own compensation scheme but that does not necessarily cover foreign investors.

Remember the Icelandic bank fiasco during the credit crunch? Thousands of individuals (including me) and even local councils and charities had put money into savings accounts run by online savings banks Icesave and Kaupthing Edge because of their fantastic savings rates. When the Icelandic banking system collapsed it seemed touch-and-go as to whether we would get our money back as their operations were only partially covered by the Financial Services Compensation Scheme (FSCS). The rest was supposed to be covered by the Icelandic government. It was only because the British government stepped in to cover deposits (in order to maintain confidence in the entire banking system) that the problem was resolved early.

In some more volatile countries where the interest rates can be quite eye-wateringly high (and I try never to cause tears) there is the risk that you may not be able to get your money out of the country. There is also a much higher risk in these countries that the financial institution you have invested in could go bust or be taken over by a new totalitarian government. Remember, too, that if you invest in another currency you could lose (or gain) due to fluctuations in exchange rates with sterling.

Many offshore accounts are multi-currency, allowing you to deposit money in various currencies. This is perfect if you travel a lot or work in more than one country and receive your wage or salary in varying currencies. But unless any of these situations apply to you, it's probably not worth bothering with an offshore account. The risks are simply too great, as your money is not protected.

---

If you travel a lot and maybe have a home in another country it makes perfect sense to set up at least a current account in that country and even a savings account or two. Often it can simply be a case of walking into a branch when you are in the country, showing your passport and setting up an account then and there. It is also possible to set up accounts online but many countries, like the UK, have increasingly strict legislation on money laundering so there will be paperwork that you have to post or show to a representative in the native country – or both.

It can be safer and easier to set up an international account with a British bank like HSBC, for example, which has branches globally.

---

# How to Get the Best Savings Rates

As you will have noticed from what I've said so far in this chapter, there are different types of savings accounts for different needs. Often the more flexibility that you get with an account, the lower the interest rate. However, even with flexible accounts you still need to make sure that you get the highest rate of interest you can.

There's no point being obsessive about chasing the best rates every week. Some people do that and they need to get a life. But it's a good idea to shop around, at least initially and then every six months or so, to find the best savings rate around. Go to the savings comparisons on Moneymagpie.com and check the savings articles on the site to find the current best buys.

When looking for the best savings rates, bear in mind that some of the best rates on offer may only last for an introductory six months or so. If that is the case then you have the choice of making a note to yourself to switch the money after six months or going for an account that has a good long-term rate that might not be as eye-catching as the initial bonus account, but at least it's pretty good for longer and will prevent you from having to chase around for good rates every six months.

The comparison site Moneyfacts.co.uk has a heading in its savings section for savings accounts with consistently best rates. These are worked out over a few years and if you're the sort of person who really can't be bothered to switch accounts every six or twelve months then go for one of those.

> **What they want you to do:** take whatever savings rate your bank/building society offers and don't move.
>
> **What you should do:** never feel any loyalty to any particular bank. Shop around for best rates at all times. Check our website, ask friends . . . Keep referring to this – your handbook to financial success!

Before you even think about investing, it's vitally important that you pay off any debts and build up enough savings. Until you do, read the advice in the rest of the book as preparation for your life as an investor but do not start investing until you've set up enough savings.

## Chapter 4

# Investing in Shares the Cheap and Easy Way

This is a BIG chapter. I'd settle down with it for an hour or so with a mug of something comforting if I were you and possibly even a notebook.

Investing in shares for the long term – and I mean long term – has historically been the best way to make your money make money. Over the last 100 years and more it has beaten all the other asset classes (including property) in terms of the average return you get on your money.

This is going to be a big chapter because there is a lot to say. In fact, entire books have been written on just small aspects of stock-market investing and entire websites and sections of newspapers are devoted to the subject with new thoughts, ideas, trends and tips coming out every day. I can't possibly hope to cover everything in detail here, but what you will find is enough information to get you started on easy and cheap stock-market investing that will help you make good money in the long term.

What I will do in this chapter is:

- *Give you an overview of what stock-market investing is and what it isn't (or what it should and shouldn't be).*
- *Explain the three different ways that you can approach investing in shares.*
- *Show you what I consider to be the easiest, cheapest and most successful way to invest without tears.*
- *Give you some basic advice on the other two methods (both are huge subjects so I will suggest where else to go for more help after giving you the basics).*

## WHAT IS THE STOCK MARKET?

The stock market (and there are various different ones around the world) is rather like your nearest street market except that instead of selling fruit, veg and cheap clothes, it sells part ownership of companies. In fact, it's probably more like an antiques market than fruit and veg because the shares it sells can be resold, either at a profit or a loss, on the same day, or weeks, months or years later.

In the UK our main stock market is known as the FTSE (pronounced 'Footsie'). That stands for the Financial Times Stock Exchange. It's the common name for a set of British stock market indices that show how well companies listed on the London Stock Exchange (LSE) are doing.

The LSE is like a big marketplace where people (and companies) come together to buy and sell shares in companies.

The FTSE All-Share is worth very roughly £1,000 billion altogether. (That is to say, if you bought all the shares for all the companies listed on the London Stock Exchange it would, in theory, cost you £1,000 billion.)

Remember, when you buy shares in a company, you actually own some of the value of that company. You may have the right to vote at shareholders' meetings, although you don't have the right actually to run the company. The company directors are there to serve the interests of the shareholders. Therefore shareholders, en masse, can influence certain acts by the company's board of directors but that usually only happens if a large portion of shareholders (usually headed by a few pension companies that own huge swathes of a company's stock) act in unison.

In the old days, the London market used to involve men coming together and yelling and waving their hands in order to buy and sell shares – this is called 'open outcry' for obvious reasons. Now everything is done by computer using fancy electronic systems. With those systems in place, it's much easier for anyone with a computer, anywhere in the world, to access the market to buy shares.

The 'index' part of 'stock market index' is simply a way of showing us how a large number of companies' shares are doing overall. The more people that like a particular company, the more they want to buy shares in it. The greater the number of people that want to buy the shares, the higher the price goes up.

If you have lots of people piling into a lot of shares in companies that are represented in an index (say, the FTSE 100), then the combined value of that index goes up. That's what they mean on the news when they say 'the FTSE 100 has gone up by 30 points', for example.

# Shares as an Asset Class

Historically shares have been the most important asset class for creating real wealth over time. People's faith in them has been severely shaken over the last decade because of the prolonged bear market (i.e. downturn in share prices) we've been going through. But then that has happened a few times before – imagine how people felt for years after the Wall Street Crash – but the market has bounced back each time.

In fact, the last decade has constituted the fourth worst 10-year period in the market since 1871. But history has shown that excellent returns come to those who have the balls to survive rough patches. Since 1871, the three worst 10-year returns for stocks have ended in the years 1920, 1974 and 1978. These were followed, respectively, by real, after-inflation returns of more than 8%, 13% and 9% over the following 10 years. In other words, hang in there (particularly when everyone else is exiting) and you'll make money in the long run.

Over the last 100 years the general trajectory of the stock-market index in this country (and in America) has been upwards. You can see in the diagram opposite how the stock market has moved over the last century (yes, I know, sorry, it's a graph but work with me on this one – it's a simple one!)

Of course, no one can predict what any investments will do for definite over the next five, ten or one hundred years. None of us has a crystal ball – least of all the investment 'experts'. However, looking at the way the stock market has moved (or 'performed' as the investment commentators like to say) in the past, it's a fairly decent bet that it will continue to do something similar over the long term, i.e. keep going up, albeit in a roller-coaster kind of a way.

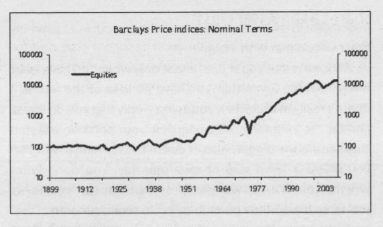

Barclays Price indices: Nominal Terms

*Source: Barclays Capital*

If you are looking to invest for the long term – i.e. you're particularly thinking of funding your retirement in 40 years' time – then shares are likely to outperform property, bonds and cash. You just need to be brave when the storms hit so don't panic and sell your shares in the middle of that time because of a temporary economic downturn.

Do remember, too, that the longer you have your money in equities (another name for shares) the more likely you are to weather the storms and make money. By 'long term' I mean at least five years or more. In fact, 10 years is a better measure of 'long term' when it comes to equities. Doing so will give you an opportunity to ride out the lows and make a good overall return (at least better than if you left your money in the bank).

Over the long term, the return you get from investing in the stock market is much the same, if not better, than the return you can get from investing in property (especially when you take the stress and costs of being a landlord into consideration) and you don't have to stump up as much initial money for an investment in shares. Some funds will let you put in £1 a month. You can't do that with a property!

My view is that you should invest only when you have spare money to risk. Given that you have no idea of the future, it doesn't really matter when you invest – only that you do invest, and for the long term. All being well, your portfolio will start small and grow bigger. Also, it doesn't really matter whether you invest a lump sum or save monthly. You don't know whether the market will go up or down in the immediate future, so there's little point in trying to time your entry.

So, be brave. Don't listen to the scared, short-term thinkers. Remember to think for yourself, do your own research, invest regularly and if you want to, be greedy when others are fearful and fearful when others are greedy (as multi-billionaire Warren Buffett says – hey, it hasn't done him any harm!)

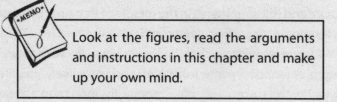

Look at the figures, read the arguments and instructions in this chapter and make up your own mind.

However, in the interests of you making your own decisions with full information, you should remember that nothing is a certainty. This is why, again, I suggest that you put just some of your money into stocks/shares (maybe just 5% of your investment money if you're unsure). The rest can go into other types of investments like property, bonds or cash. It's up to you and it all depends on what you can feel comfortable with. There's no point investing in something if it will keep you awake at night.

# Fundamental Principles of Stock-Market Investing

The fundamental principles of investing in the stock market are similar to those of investing generally.

## THINK FOR YOURSELF

Most importantly you should do your own reading and research, look at the fundamental value of companies (or shares-based products like tracker funds or other stock-market funds) rather than what's in fashion and make your own decisions.

## THINK LONG TERM

Proper stock-market investing isn't about gambling or speculating. It's about ownership – buying stakes in well-managed businesses in order to profit from their ongoing success. Buy them in order to hold on to them for years . . . and years . . . and years . . .

## HOLD TIGHT

. . . and be aware that during those years the stock market, and the individual companies you invest in, will go up and down. You need to be strong and look to the long term rather than being spooked by short-term changes. The best stock-market investors are those who have done their research, made sure that the results of that research still hold true, stand strong, will hold their nerve and not be swayed by the panic or the misplaced enthusiasm going on around them.

## BE A CONTRARIAN

What most people do with the stock market is they wait until everyone is piling into shares, or perhaps piling into a particular sector of the market, and when that market is really high and it's actually quite expensive to buy, then they invest. Shortly after that the market peaks and starts to drop like a stone. When their investment is worth quite a lot less than they put in originally then these people are so scared and disappointed that they pull out.

Do the opposite. When the market or your favourite share plunges, that's when you buy – assuming, based upon the in-depth research you have done on that company, you think that the underlying, fundamental value of it is sound. If the real value is sound then, in time, the scare or fashion that made it go down will evaporate and it will climb again. If you're looking to sell your shares then the time to do it is when everyone is buying and you feel the price is more than it really should be.

## SET SOME RULES FOR YOURSELF

That rule might be simply to buy and hold until you retire. If that's the one you like then fine, go for it. That's largely the way I operate (described by Robbie Burns in *The Naked Trader* as 'Mrs Buy and Hold' – it's a typically female approach, apparently, and has one of the highest chances of success as an investing strategy). Just make sure you stick to it even in bad markets.

Another rule, as suggested by my friend Campbell Edgar of wealth managers Andersen Charnley, is to set yourself a percentage of your money that you want to keep in shares, for example, and stick to that. This means that if you have, say, 70%

of your money in shares and they go up in value, you will automatically have a higher percentage in them after a while. This is because the value has gone up. So as your holdings go up in value you may find that soon you actually have 80% of your money in shares, simply because their value has gone up that much. At that point you should sell the extra 10%, put that money in cash or bonds and you are back to 70%. This, in many cases, will have the same effect as selling when the shares are valuable and then buying when they are cheap (because if the stock market performs worse than the other parts of your investment portfolio then the portion of your portfolio in share holdings will have gone down to, say, 60% so you would invest in shares to bring the portion back up to your target – in this instance 70%).

## KEEP INFORMED

You don't have to spend all your time scouring the columns in the *FT* every day, but it is a good idea for everyone who is serious about investing at least a little bit to keep themselves generally informed about the markets and about investing principles. I have put suggestions of websites, publications and books on pages 118–19 so pick a few that you like the look of (including, of course, the Moneymagpie articles and newsletter) and go through those.

## BE REGULAR

Don't try to 'time the market' as many stock-pickers try to do. In other words, don't wait and wait and wait for the market to get to a certain level before you put money in. It doesn't work like that unless you are dedicated to studying a sector and being able to spot undervalued companies. Some people think they can predict what the market will do but they're always wrong. There are too many variables for anyone to do it accurately. So go for solid, regular investing, either every month or once or twice a year, whenever you get the money in. By investing regularly you will catch the ups and downs, the cheap times and the expensive times at roughly the same rates so that over time you will buy shares at a decent, average rate (it's called 'pound cost averaging' in the trade).

## When Do You Sell?

Many 'stock-pickers' (people who invest in individual shares) try to 'time the market'. In other words, they try to work out when shares are at their cheapest in order to buy them and when they're at their peak in order to sell. Most of the time they fail because, even with clever graphs and calculations, it's pretty much impossible to time the market accurately. The market is just not a very logical creature and most of the time it won't play ball.

Generally speaking, for most amateur investors, you're better off simply buying into the stock market regularly (say every month or at least a few times a year) and keeping what you've bought for years and years until you want to retire. Yes, you will suffer big drops in your portfolio as the stock market lurches down every now and then but overall you will gain.

More sophisticated investors see signs of the market becoming a bubble and they take most (though usually not all) of their money out before it bursts. This is the same with the property market, by the way. It's not just the stock market that suffers big ups and downs. Different people have different ways of spotting this but in general, when everyone is piling into the market, there are TV programmes about it, people are talking about it at dinner parties and you realise that people are paying silly money for things that really aren't worth the price, those are good indications that a market is over-heating and will crash soon. If you have the confidence, this is the time to pull out at least some of your money.

## 'YES, BUT WHAT ABOUT THE HUGE CRASHES IN THE MARKET? WON'T I LOSE EVERYTHING?'

Not if you're investing for the long term and have created a diverse (that word again) portfolio.

As I said above, on a daily basis, even on an hourly basis, the stock market can go up and down faster than a meerkat on speed. Sometimes – such as the Wall Street Crash in the late-1920s, the mid-1970s when there was the oil crisis, just after 9/11, and in 2008 as a result of a build-up of poor lending and borrowing decisions – there have been big dives and everyone has been very frightened for a time.

However, if you put the papers aside, take a calm, deep breath and step back, you will see that the long-term view is quite different. Because although the stock market can go up and down wildly even in one day, over time those ups and downs are smoothed out and the losses are more than made up for by the gains.

Nothing is certain, of course, which is why I say diversify.

However, as I have explained above, even long bear markets (like the 10-year one to 2008) have historically been followed by good bull markets where losses have been more than made up sooner or later. Stick in there and the gains should come in.

## Three Ways to Invest

As with investing in general, investing in the stock market can be divided into three approaches:

- *No responsibility at all – either give it to expensive brokers (if you're a wealthy family/individual and can't be bothered) who may or may not choose the right stocks and funds; or let your bank/financial adviser do it all for you, investing in managed products that are going to do badly.*
- *Total responsibility – become a stock-picker choosing stocks to buy and sell, trying to time the market, trying to create the right mix of securities investments.*
- *Partial responsibility – keep an eye on trends and have some knowledge of the markets and invest in tracker funds, ETFs and possibly move on to buying (and holding) a few blue-chip shares, only buying when they look undervalued.*

And it's the third method of investing that I am going to start with because in my opinion, this is the simplest, cheapest and most successful way for ordinary people (like me) to make money long term. This is what I do mostly with my money.

# Partial Responsibility

If, like me, you have a life and you don't have the time or interest to spend days, months, years studying the market in order to pick the right shares to invest in, but (rightly) you don't trust fund managers or stockbrokers to do it for you either, then I suggest you opt for this method of investing first.

It's not a completely hands-off approach. You do have to think about it, read up a little and decide each year where you are going to put your money (in terms of which fund, which index, which country, etc.), but it's nothing like the level of thought and energy you have to put in to actual stock-picking.

So, my preferred method is to build up a good collection of index trackers and ETFs first and then later (possibly much later) if you're really interested, and you have developed a lot of knowledge, you can get into stock-picking – i.e. investing in specific shares – and maybe you will find some decent managed funds (there are a few) along the way and decide to put some cash there too.

However, right now, if you want to beat the banks, make money and still have loads of time to spare for yourself, I would invest in a range of index-tracking funds and ETFs. Here's what they are and how to do it.

## INDEX-TRACKING FUNDS

*Skill level: beginner*

Tracker funds 'track' a particular stock-market index (i.e. defined group of companies such as the largest 100) by investing some of your money in every single company in that index. This means that as the index goes up or down (depending on how the shares of each of the companies in the index do each day), your investment goes up and down with it.

There are various 'indices' in Britain and around the world that are 'tracked' by tracker funds. For example, the 'FTSE 100' (the index you keep hearing about in the news) is made up of the 100 biggest companies that have shares available to buy and sell on the London Stock Exchange (LSE) – that's where those shares are 'listed'.

When a company gets 'listed' on a stock market it means that at least part of it has been sold to the public (i.e. you, me or anyone else who wants to buy those shares) rather than being privately owned.

In other words, lots of people can own a little bit of each company by buying one or more bits – 'shares' – of it. Once a company is listed it can only become a 'private' company again if it buys back all of the shares or if another company or group of people does so and thereby 'de-lists' the company – this is what Richard Branson did with his company, Virgin.

If you are considering investing in a tracker fund or two, another index you should be familiar with is the FTSE All-Share, which represents the vast majority of companies that are listed on the London Stock Exchange (over 700 of them).

There's also nothing to stop you investing in a fund that tracks one of the many other indices, such as AIM (the Alternative Investment Market which is the market for smaller companies in the UK), the Dow Jones or the Nasdaq in America, the Nikkei in Japan, the Hang Seng in Hong Kong or the DAX in Germany – in fact I suggest that in time you should spread your money across different countries and sectors – but to start with, stick to British funds where you know where you are and you have easier access to information about them.

## THE DIFFERENT TYPES OF INDICES TO TRACK

There are three main British indices that you can choose to 'track'. The FTSE 100 and the FTSE All-Share tend to perform pretty similarly, but the third, the FTSE 250, goes up and down a little more because it's made up of middle-sized companies, for which the prices can be a bit more volatile.

The FTSE 100 – The FTSE 100 measures the largest 100 companies in the UK by value. One current example is BP, which is UK-based, but operates internationally.

The top 100 companies represent about 80% of the value of the whole of the London-based market (the FTSE All-Share), so you can get a pretty good idea of what the stock market as a whole is doing from how these top 100 companies are performing. This is why they report on the FTSE 100 in the news – if the FTSE 100 is up a few points then the overall feeling is positive and companies are generally perceived to be doing well.

The FTSE 250 – The next 250 biggest companies in size are known as the FTSE 250 – in other words, the companies ranked 101 to 350 in the market. Companies in this index are generally known as the 'mid-caps', meaning that they have a capitalisation (what they would be worth if you sold them) that is somewhere in the middle between the FTSE 100 and all the other tiddly little companies that are listed.

Interestingly, many of the traditionally 'British' companies, like manufacturers and house-building companies, are often found in the FTSE 250. For that reason, investors often choose to track this index if they believe the next few years will be bright for the British economy. They'll look for signals such as a falling unemployment rate, which means more people are holding down jobs and able to spend more on housing, travel and shopping.

The FTSE All-Share – The FTSE All-Share measures how the major part of the companies (around 700 of them) listed on the London Stock Exchange is doing. This includes each one that sells shares to the public, from the very big household names like BT to the tiddlers, such as estate agents. Although it includes all of the publicly listed companies in the country it moves up and down in a similar way to the FTSE 100 because the first 100 companies in the index account for the vast majority of the wealth of the whole lot.

## How to invest in an index-tracking fund (tracker fund)

It's very simple to invest in an index-tracking fund. You can apply by phone, post or online. Just ring the company you like that offers tracker funds (there's a list of them on page 318), tell them that you want to put some money into a tracker fund, and they will send you a form to fill in and sign.

You send it back to them with a cheque (or even pay with a credit card over the phone or online) together with documentation that shows you are who you say you are (money-laundering rules) and you're done. They will ask you if you would like the fund wrapped in an ISA, so if you haven't already used up your ISA allowance this tax year, you can do that and you're saving tax as well.

You can invest online as well. Just go to the tracker fund company's website (there's a list of them on page 318), look for the section on funds and search through for index-tracking funds. All the websites have different ways of displaying their information, so it might take a minute or so to find the part for index-tracking funds. Once you do, it's pretty straightforward.

It's a good idea to have a look at their website first and search for reviews online (check Moneymagpie.com and Fool.co.uk for info) to see what kinds of tracker funds the company operates. Most investment companies have funds that invest in different indices around the world. It's entirely up to you which one you invest in and how much you put in them.

Remember, you should spread your money over different types of investments, so think about how confident you are in the stock market long term. If you like the idea of it, and if you are planning to keep your money in a particular investment for at least five years (really ten years or more is even better) then go for it.

It's a good idea to put money in different funds and different countries over the years to spread your investments around, but if you have never invested in a stock market before, then I suggest you invest in the UK one to start off with.

There's nothing to stop you investing in one type of tracker (say the FTSE 100) one year with one company (say, M&G) and then another type the next year (say, the FTSE All-Share) with another company (say, Fidelity) and so on.

After three or four years, you could start getting adventurous with investments in an American index tracker or the FTSE 250 or the DAX in Germany. Your choice will depend on your research – on which market looks promising for the long term.

There's not a lot to tell between the performance of different companies' tracker funds in Britain; most do roughly the same. However, some charge more in management fees than others, so you're probably best off going for the ones with low annual management charges (i.e. 1.5% or below).

Interestingly, economists say that the factor that is most likely to affect your investment is the annual management charges. The higher they are, on the whole, the worse your investment will do over time. So, as a general rule, if all other factors are equal, go for the fund or investment that has the lowest annual charges.

## EXCHANGE-TRADED FUNDS – ETFs

*Skill level: beginner to intermediate*

I like exchange-traded funds: they're cheap, pretty easy to buy and sell, and they work. They haven't been around for very long, so people are only just beginning to catch on to them.

ETFs aren't managed by a fund manager (i.e. 'actively' managed). Like trackers, they're 'passive' funds, so they're less expensive as there aren't any management fees or commission. In fact, there are often even fewer fees for ETFs than there are for trackers.

ETFs are like traditional 'tracker' funds, meaning that they copy the performance of a market, such as the FTSE 100, for their own value. They also track entire countries (you can buy a China ETF or a Brazil ETF if you think those countries are going to experience economic growth), they track commodities such as oil, zinc and pigs and they also track bonds (as you can find out in Chapter 6).

Unlike tracker funds, though, exchange-traded funds are actual companies in their own right and they're traded like individual shares. So they're actual companies which do nothing but put lots of money into tracker funds and you buy shares in the company itself. Their value simply reflects the value of their underlying investment, usually one index or another.

In order to buy or sell a share in them you have to set up an account with a broker, just like you would if you wanted to buy shares in BT or Tesco. I suggest you set up an account with a nice, cheap online broker as I explain overleaf.

You only have to buy one share to be involved in the fund (obviously the shares differ in price). They're very flexible too, and you can leave your investment in for as long or as short a time as you like, just like you can with trackers.

## Why are ETFs a good investment?

They're cheap. Investment specialists say that one of the biggest factors affecting the health of your investments is the annual charges. Economists have worked out that when the charges are low it really helps your fund grow each year, mainly because less is taken out each year so you have more money in there to grow.

They are simple. There aren't lots of complicated layers and structures in them. They just invest directly into a stock-market index or into a specific commodity (like oil or sugar or steel), bonds or even into a particular country.

There's lots to choose from. ETFs can be bought for exotic markets as well as British ones, such as Brazil, Eastern Europe,

Taiwan or Korea, which have previously been rather hard to invest in for ordinary investors like us.

They work. ETFs are getting more popular because they have been proven to make money quite cheaply.

**How do I invest in an ETF?**

First, you'll need to set up an account with a stockbroker and I suggest you go for an online one. It's free to register with online brokers and you don't have to buy anything immediately once you have your account.

You can join now and wait for months before you invest in anything. However, once you do trade, it will be very cheap to buy and sell ETFs and you will have constant access to your stock.

There are online brokers now including:

- *TD Waterhouse: charge from £9.95 per online trade (Tdwaterhouse.co.uk, 0845 6076002)*
- *Selftrade: £12.50 per trade – online, by telephone or via your mobile – and just £6 per trade when you qualify for its Frequent Trader scheme (Selftrade.co.uk, 0845 0700720)*
- *Halifax Share Dealing: deal online for £11.95 (excluding international deals) or over the telephone from £15 (Halifax.co.uk, 0845 7225525)*

NB These prices are correct at the time of writing (December 2009).

Once you have an account, you can credit it with a money transfer, invest in your ETF, and start to make some investments that will pay dividends!

## Then choose your ETF

The ETFs that most people buy in the UK are those produced by iShares, which are index-tracking funds. In other words, they track a particular stock-market index. If you look on the iShares site (Ishares.com) and click on the 'iShares funds' button you will see a list of all the funds they offer.

The most common iShare in the UK at the moment is the iFTSE 100, which tracks the FTSE 100 index. Another one that people invest in a lot is iShares S&P 500, which tracks the S&P 500 index in the United States – the 500 largest companies listed on the New York Stock Exchange.

If you were interested in investing in an economy like Brazil (it being fairly buoyant at the time of writing), you could consider the iShares MSCI Brazil fund. There are several different areas to choose from. It depends on what your research tells you is going to grow over the coming months and years.

Once you have decided which one you want to invest in, make a note of the code for that fund (it can be found on the search function of the website of the broker that you're using) and look for it in the list of the online broker you have chosen. So, for example, the iShares FTSE 100 ETF has the ticker 'ISF' and their Brazil fund is 'IBZL'. Or the ETF Securities Short Crude Oil fund (one of the ones you could invest in if you wanted to follow oil, for example) has the ticker 'SOIL'.

When you go to your online broker account, you put this code in when it asks you what you want to buy. The online broker should confirm the full name of the fund (or individual company) before you go ahead and buy into it.

## Beware of 'derivative', 'leveraged' and 'short' ETFs

There are two main types of exchange-traded funds: asset-backed funds and derivative-based funds.

Asset-backed funds are the safe option, and simply track a market. Then there are derivative-based funds. As their name implies, they use derivatives to track a market or product. This is where the fund enters into an agreement with another firm (such as an investment bank) to provide a return on the investment, based on, say, gold price movements (often putting investors' money into bonds).

The risk with these types of funds is that you are reliant on the organisation the fund is partnered with being in good financial health. If they go bust, it's usually curtains for your fund – and any money you had invested in it.

It also pays to be extremely wary of so-called 'leveraged' or 'short' ETFs that some funds promote to try to get increased returns from the market.

A 'leveraged' ETF works by leveraging the profits (and the risks). For example, it may offer a 2% rise for every 1% rise in an index – but if the markets fell, you would lose 2% for every 1% fall.

A 'short' ETF, meanwhile, acts as a sort of reverse bet against the market. For instance, a short ETF could offer a 2% rise for every 1% fall in an index. But if the market rose, you would lose 2% for every 1% rise.

These short and leveraged funds are suited to short-term investment bets, but are not recommended as they expose you to potentially huge losses. It was just these sorts of funds that played such a fatal role in the financial crisis, as companies and banks were forced to default on payments. Indeed, some banks have stopped trading short and leveraged funds because of the damage they have caused.

It's far better to stick with a non-leveraged, plain old 'vanilla' asset-backed exchange-traded fund (like iShares FTSE100 or ETFS Gold Bullion Securities). These offer a slower, steadier investment approach but are infinitely less risky.

Once you have invested your money in a tracker fund or an ETF, you can pretty much forget about it apart from when you get a report on your investment from the company – usually twice a year. Some years, your money will have increased, other years it will have gone down, depending on how the index itself did that year.

Remember, you need to have your money in that investment for at least five years to get any real benefit from it. Over the long term these funds have historically gone up, even though at times they looked shaky. Hang in there!

## DO IT IN AN ISA

As I mention in Chapter 8, you can save a lot of money over time by using ISAs – tax-saving wrappers – to protect your money from tax. ISAs are not products in themselves, they're like wrappers into which you put an investment and that wrapper stops you having to pay tax on anything you make.

With a cash ISA, effectively you set up a savings account (with a building society or bank) but when you get your interest, the government won't take tax out of it.

With shares ISAs, if your investment grows, you won't be taxed on that growth. We all have an ISA allowance each tax year (6 April Year One to 5 April Year Two), which is essentially a limit on how much money you can contribute to your ISA in any single tax year.

ISAs were set up to encourage people to invest for the long term, which is why the government allows us to put the full ISA allowance into shares but only half that amount into cash. This is because the government knows that long-term shares offer us a much better chance of making money for our retirement than cash does.

It's up to you how you put money into your shares ISA. You can put it into a tracker fund and ask for it to be wrapped in an ISA, or you can put it in a managed fund (page 120), an ETF (page 104) or individual shares; just ask whoever is organising the investment to wrap it in an ISA for you.

Or you could have what's called a 'self-select ISA' where you get an ISA 'wrapper' and then choose either individual shares or a combination of funds to put inside it. However, if you haven't even started investing in the stock market yet I wouldn't worry about that. Just go for a simpler investment that can come pre-wrapped in an ISA, like tracker funds. You can find out how to get these products on page 318.

There are other tax-saving gizmos that you can use to save money on your investments and I'll cover some of them in Chapter 8. However, some of them, such as VCTs, EISs and REITs, have done so badly on the whole that even with the tax saving I consider that it's still not worth investing in them.

## WHAT TO DO ONCE YOU HAVE MADE YOUR INVESTMENT IN TRACKERS OR ETFs . . .

Once you finish the application, you will be sent paper forms to fill in and you will probably need to show that you are who you say you are (anti-money-laundering legislation insists on that). That will mean sending some household bills and your passport or driving licence, which they will return.

Then once the money is in there, you can do one of three things:

- *Keep an eye on it daily, weekly or monthly, wondering whether you should pull out now or buy more or switch to something else, etc.*
- *Ignore it mostly but try to time the market, noticing when you think shares generally have peaked and taking all or most of your money out before that happens and putting it in cash or another asset class.*
- *Leave it, leave it and leave it until about five years before you are planning on retiring, when you should start to move your money out and into more stable investments such as bonds. This is called 'lifestyling', where you take the gains you have made over the long term but now you're looking at short-term investing, so you need to have your money in something stable that won't suddenly drop right down just as you want to retire.*

Me? I'm a 'leave it' investor. I will move money out of investments if I'm sure I can see a bubble forming but on the whole (and partly because I have better things to do with my time) I think the best policy is to leave my money in these investments for as long as possible to let them grow in their own sweet way.

Of course, there is nothing to stop you moving your money about before this time. You can take your money out and put it in something else any time you want. However, if you do, make sure it's for the right reasons and make sure you have given your investments long enough to grow and take advantage of the upswings in the market as well as coping with the downswings.

Make sure, too, that you are not spooked by market crashes and take your money out of a tracker fund in panic when it is right at the bottom. If you did that, you really would lose out. Personally, when I see the market crashing, I look on it as an opportunity to buy more, not to sell. When everyone else is selling in panic, that's when I decide to go in and put more money in (if I have some spare cash) while it is nice and cheap.

## More information

I recommend that you do some further reading before you take the plunge.

- *Start with the articles in the 'investing' section of Moneymagpie.com.*
- *Read what the Motley Fool has to say about tracker funds and ETFs (and general investing strategies) at Fool.co.uk.*
- *Read* A Random Walk Down Wall Street *by Burton Malkiel, which argues the case for index trackers vs stock-picking.*

> **What they want you to do:** invest in the well-advertised, expensive, managed funds that bring good money in for the fund managers but often actually lose money for you.
> **What you should do:** avoid these until you have created a solid base of investments in tracker funds and ETFs (see page 99) and then only try a few of these if you think they are genuinely good and have lower charges.

# Total Responsibility

## STOCK-PICKING

*Skill level: advanced and very advanced*

It might sound daft to say this but stock-picking can be a lot of fun. Stock-picking means that you buy shares of individual companies (like Shell or HSBC or Boots or Marks & Spencer) and then sell them at some point to make a profit. You might also invest in stock-market funds but primarily you are interested in individual companies and you will try to find ones where their shares will go up in time so that you will make money.

If you're actually interested in business, in the way markets work, in a particular sector of the economy or a particular part of the world, researching and investing in individual companies (stocks) can be a good way of finding out more about these things. For some people it's a lucrative hobby.

However, given that you are putting actual money in – your actual money that you, or someone who loved you, worked hard for – it's also a potentially scary thing to do. If you're going to do it properly you're going to have to put in yet more hard work.

Also, to make it worthwhile, you're going to need to pick shares that, over the long term, out-perform the stock market generally. In other words, you will have to invest in a collection of companies that, together, make you more money than you would have made by just buying into a bunch of tracker funds.

This means that, before tax and inflation, you need to be making more than 10% a year on average to make it worth it.

It is possible to do it: after all, that's how Warren Buffett has made his billions. He is one, by the way, who very much believes in buying for the long term. As far as he is concerned, and you should be concerned, stock-market investing isn't about gambling or speculating. It's about ownership – buying stakes in well-managed businesses in order to profit from their ongoing success.

You could try being a trader from home. That was very popular in the 1990s when the markets were very buoyant and you could make money just by being lucky. Now, though, reality has set in for long enough to put most people off the practice, other than a few hardened gambling types.

## Get a strategy

The stock market is so big and so diverse that if you want to go down the stock-picking route you need to have a strategy and limit yourself only to looking at certain types of companies, whether that be companies in one sector only (pharmaceuticals, retail, oil and gas, for example) or companies that meet certain criteria.

There are a few well-known investing strategies that are followed by professional and amateur investors. It's up to you which one suits your personality best. Each has its own pros and cons. Here are the main ones for you to choose from:

- *Growth. You buy shares that you believe will grow in the long term.*
- *Value investing. This is a type of investing that makes a lot of sense. The idea is that you buy shares that are cheap and then reap rewards as they grow exponentially. This is worth doing if you have spent a long time (probably years) watching a particular company and you know what you think it's worth. Once it drops in price (perhaps because that sector has gone out of favour generally) and you still think it's a sound company, you buy the shares. Value investing was first proposed by Benjamin Graham and David Dodd and is the method that Warren Buffett uses to invest.*

  *It's a principle that makes sense: if you know (or think you know) how much a company is worth and you see that it is valued at much lower than that, you would expect it to make money if bought at that discount price.*
- *Sector-specific investing. With this you research one particular sector, or even part of a sector, in-depth so that you know everything there is to know about it and can make really informed decisions about which companies to invest in. It's a good idea to pick a sector that you either work in (maybe you work in retail, for example, and already know a lot about it) or you are interested in (such as a friend of mine who is fascinated by the geo-politics of the oil and gas industry and follows that avidly).*

- *Top-down investing. This is similar to sector investing where you find a sector (such as companies dealing in water or waste management) that you think will do well in the near future because of world trends then you pick the best companies in that area. If you have an idea of what will be the 'next big thing', then you can get one step ahead of the competition and enjoy enhanced returns. For example, the biggest gains from the late-1990s dot-com boom came to those who arrived early to the party, while those who jumped on the bandwagon too late suffered huge losses.*

  *Try exploring some of the 'big picture' themes to help shape your portfolio. For example, factors such as population growth and the emergence of China as a world superpower will play a big part in our economic future. Therefore, those who choose to invest in solid companies with long-term futures in industries such as agriculture, infrastructure, utilities, water and waste management could reap big rewards.*

- *Charting. If you're a total number-crunching geek you might enjoy this form of investing, which uses price charts and other technical data to predict what will happen in the markets in the future. It's not my thing and I don't honestly think it works but many books have been written about why devotees think it does!*

## How to think

As I have said before in this chapter, the basic of any sort of successful investing is getting your thinking right. Here are a few pointers on how to approach stock-picking:

Don't rush in. Genuinely successful investors have been doing it for years and years. Really it's a good idea to be reading, researching and, probably, running a virtual portfolio (also known as paper trading) – Yahoo does one – where you don't have to lose your own money for at least two years before you actually put any of your own hard-earned into even one company. Essentially you do all the research and reading you would do if you were actually buying shares and you then pretend to buy and sell them but it's like doing it with Monopoly money. You see the numbers and how much you would have made, or lost, but you don't actually use your own hard-earned cash at all.

Learn from mistakes – yours and other people's. Face it, you can't make an omelette without breaking eggs and you're going to make some bad decisions when you start investing. So long as you are open enough, honest enough and humble enough to recognise when you've been silly, rash, hoodwinked, etc., then you can learn from those (often expensive) mistakes and move on.

Be bold. Once you have made your decision that a particular company is brilliant, buy big. Also, only buy a few companies – five or six is probably the maximum you should aim to start with. The more companies you hold and the more diversified your portfolio, the more it is likely simply to mirror the stock-market index, in which case you would be better off (in terms of time and effort) just investing in a basic index tracker. If you're going to stock-pick you should make it pay by finding the golden nuggets and going for the big time.

Be disciplined. It's a good idea to be open to accepting that you might have got it horribly wrong and getting out while the going is good, once in a while, but make sure you are getting out for the right reasons. On the whole, if you have done your thorough research and you have invested because you honestly believe a company is going to do well in the long term then stick with your strategy and ignore the comments, advice and hysteria that can come in from the media, analysts and your investing buddies. As Ben Graham, the father of Value Investing, said: 'You are neither right nor wrong because the crowd disagrees with you. You are right because your data and reasoning are right.'

Get informed and stay informed. Having said that you shouldn't take too much notice of what others around you are saying or doing about the company, sector or strategy you are into, it's also important to keep abreast of economic developments here and abroad, to know what the trends are now and likely to be and also to be aware of new, and old, academic thinking on investment strategy.

Obviously you should be signed up to the free Moneymagpie newsletter (the sign-up box is on the home page of Moneymagpie.com) which often has tips on saving and investing. Also get into the Motley Fool (Fool.co.uk) and Interactive Investor (Iii.co.uk) for regular articles and infomation on investing strategies and stock tips. Definitely read the *Financial Times*, either online or on paper, and check out Citiwire.co.uk and the magazine *Investor's Chronicle*.

I subscribe to the economist John Kay's blog at Johnkay.com as I consider he speaks a lot of sense. For some informative, and often humorous, reading I also recommend Warren Buffett's annual letters to shareholders on his website www.berkshire hathaway.com/letters/letters.html.

Before you even start investing seriously, though, you should read and digest a few seminal works on the subject. Here is just a handful to get you started (there are many, many more to choose from!):

- The Intelligent Investor *by Benjamin Graham. This book pioneered the concept of making money through undervalued shares.*
- Contrarian Investment Strategies *by David Dreman argues for shorter-term investments in lowly rated companies.*
- The Naked Trader *by Robbie Burns is for dedicated investor types who hanker for the cut-and-thrust of trading from home . . . in your pants (you don't have to do it in your pants but you could if you liked – that seems to be part of the attraction).*
- Common Stocks and Uncommon Profits *by Philip Fisher is good for showing you how to spot new companies that could grow fast as trends change in the world. This is good if you are interested in AIM companies or the top-down investing strategy mentioned above.*

## How to buy into individual companies

Once you have found one or two companies you want to invest in you should sign up with an online brokerage company. You can't just go ahead and ring up the companies themselves and ask to buy their shares.

Shares are sold through an intermediary known as a broker and the cheapest type is an 'execution only' (i.e. they don't give you any advice, they just do what you say) online broker. I have given you a list of possible online brokers to join on page 106 (in the ETFs section) and page 317 so pick the one that you think would be the cheapest all round for you and join (they charge roughly the same but some are cheaper than others if you plan on buying and selling shares a lot in the next year).

Then you need to have the company's code to hand, look for it on the broker's site and send a request to buy, transferring in as much money as you want to pay.

If you want to save tax on these investments you can put them in a 'self-select' ISA which is like a tax-saving bag into which you put the shares you want. There is a limit to the amount you can put into an ISA each tax year (find out what this year's limit is at the HMRC website hmrc.gov.uk) but you can keep the money in your ISA for as long as you like once you've invested in it. With 'self-select' ISAs, you can put different investments into the 'bag' and all of them benefit from being protected from tax. It's a good way to invest as you make more money in the long run.

# No Responsibility

## MANAGED FUNDS AND WEALTH MANAGEMENT COMPANIES

*Skill level: beginner to intermediate*

This is the lazy person's way of investing. It can often turn out to be the poorer person's way as many managers, advisers and brokers do a very bad job at a high fee. It's an unpleasant fact but a fact nonetheless. Keep it in mind if you do decide to take one on.

Admittedly, for some people, particularly those who are so wealthy and so busy they really don't have the time to manage their own money, it can be a help to have a true professional running your money. However, you're giving your money to people who don't have your best interests at heart, even if you're a client. It's not their personal money so they have less of a vested interest in making it work. On the other hand, this approach can give you access to high-net-worth investments such as hedge funds, private equity, investment partnerships, etc., which might do very well (or could completely bomb, remember that!)

Do keep at the forefront of your mind, though, if you go down the 'no responsibility route' you will pay. Managed funds, special packaged-up investments, funds of funds, hedge funds and the rest charge fees, sometimes high fees (there are products that will charge you up to 7% before investing your money).

## GET AN INDEPENDENT FINANCIAL ADVISER/FINANCIAL PLANNER (NOT MUCH EFFORT BUT SOME COST)

If you really want to you could get yourself an independent financial adviser. Make sure it's one who charges you for their time and lets you know what they're being paid in commissions – ideally nothing so they are not swayed by commission but by what's best for you. Take their advice as to which stock-market funds and other investments you should get into.

Good financial advisers (personally I prefer 'financial planners' to advisers as they are less product-based in their approach) will suggest tracker funds and ETFs to you as well as, or instead of, managed funds.

However, the majority will be far more enamoured of managed funds because:

- *They don't know much (seriously, I've seen the courses they do – they really don't know much).*
- *Managed funds bombard them with advertising and marketing material.*
- *They get much better commissions from managed products than from passive ones.*

On the whole, if you're going to go for a financial adviser, even if it's just for a few specific things like pension planning or you're wondering how to cut down on the tax in your investments, you should only go for:

- *Genuinely independent advisers – those who can offer products from the whole of the market, not those who are tied to one or two companies. All you need to do to find out if they have access to the whole of the market is to ask them. It's a simple question – yes or no!*
- *Advisers who are recommended to you by people whose views you trust.*

If you don't know where to start, go to Unbiased.co.uk for a list of independent financial advisers in your area.

Even if you do go down this route, it's still a good idea to get clued up about investments beforehand. Ask the adviser why they have made particular recommendations and why they haven't made others. At the very least it will keep them on their toes and make them realise they can't just sell you anything.

Go to Appendix 2 (page 315) for advice on how to find a good, independent financial adviser or financial planner.

# FIND A 'STAR FUND MANAGER' AND STICK WITH THEM (MORE EFFORT AND SOME COST)

More than three-quarters of managed funds (these include mostly unit trusts and investments trusts) underperform the stock market, i.e. a tracker fund that automatically follows the ups and downs of, say, the FTSE 100 will give you a better return than a managed fund run by an 'expert'. However, there are still a few that beat the FTSE and sometimes beat it very well.

So if some of them are beating the market really well why wouldn't you want a piece of that – even factoring in the high charges these funds often levy? Well, the main reason is because it's almost impossible to predict which funds will do well. I say almost impossible because there are a few funds run by what are called 'star fund managers' that perform consistently well at least for a few years. Those who like to invest in managed funds hunt around to find these people and will follow them around as they move, sometimes, from company to company.

Currently, while I'm writing at the end of 2009, top fund managers who are good at averaging a better return than the market are Neil Woodford at Invesco Perpetual and Anthony Bolton (formerly of Fidelity). But (and this is a big but) do be aware that past performance is no guide to the future. There's some evidence to suggest the worst-performing funds often continue to do badly, perhaps due to a poor manager or strategy, or because of high charges.

**So why bother?**
Good question – there aren't many reasons. Most really aren't worth wasting your time on.

If you can find a fund manager who 'eats his own cooking' by keeping most of his wealth in his fund, which is what Buffett does with Berkshire Hathaway, then that's one to take seriously. In fact, there's nothing to stop you investing in Berkshire Hathaway itself, other than lack of cash (one share in his company will set you back over $100,000) but even if you can't afford one of those shares, if you find another fund manager who is successful and invests in his own fund, that may be worth considering.

## GET A 'FULL-SERVICE' STOCKBROKER (LITTLE EFFORT, LOT OF COST)

A full-service broker is essentially a one-stop shop for all of your financial needs. They're like upmarket financial advisers (with upmarket fees to match) and they advise their clients on all manner of money matters including tax issues and retirement plans as well as managing your investments and trading on your behalf. To be fair, they can be good for people with so much cash and so little time that outsourced, professional portfolio management is the only option.

Remember, every time they trade it costs you money but makes money for them. Guess what – they like to trade a lot on your behalf. Really, these people are not worth looking at unless you have a big pot of cash, little time to manage your own financial affairs and a lot of trust you are willing to place in men in suits who holiday in Mustique several times a year.

However, for most people (and I certainly include myself in this) they're just an expensive way of allowing other people to make mistakes on your behalf. You're much better off sticking with tracker funds and ETFs.

You can get more in-depth, practical advice on how to invest for yourself and beat the system through the Moneymagpie Investing Workshops and the Moneymagpie Managing your Money Seminars. Go to www.moneymagpie.com/workshops to find out when the next ones are happening and how to enrol.

## Chapter 5

# Pensions – Not the Be-All and End-All of Your Retirement Fund but a Damned Good Start!

'Pension' – awful word. It just reeks of age and everything unglamorous. Who would want something so depressing?

Not only that but there have been so many stories in the last few years about pensions doing badly, mis-selling scandals, company pensions disappearing and so on that many people are, understandably, suspicious of any sort of pension now.

However, let's be clear what a pension is: it's basically just another type of investment. It's an investment with special rules, particularly special tax rules, governing it. When you contribute to a pension, the government adds in the tax you would have paid on that money. So if you're a standard-rate taxpayer, for every 80p you put into your pension, the government adds in another 20p. Also, money you put into a pension cannot be touched until you have reached a certain age. On the one hand this is annoying and restrictive, but on the other hand it protects you from yourself and makes sure that you have at least something to keep you going when you retire other than the paltry state pension (see page 130 for information on that).

For years pensions have been seen as the main way – often the only way – to save for your retirement, but actually they're only one of various different products you could put your money in for your future. They just happen to be particularly well suited to saving for retirement. There are other investments you could and should make for your retirement but those generally don't have the advantageous tax rules that pensions enjoy. Also, because you run them, you could take some of the money out and spend it, thus robbing your future self of some handy cash. In fact, that's really the point of this book – to show you the different, good products you can put your money into for your future.

You absolutely don't have to have a pension as part of your 'retirement fund' but if you a) have a job in a company that offers a contributory company pension or b) think you might be undisciplined and would dip into investments if left to your own devices or c) want to go for a range of different invest-ments for your retirement portfolio then you should definitely have at least one pension, if not more, in your pot.

# Reality Check

So let's get one disturbing fact absolutely straight:

The pension you get from the government (i.e. your state pension) will not be enough to live off.

No matter how long you've been paying taxes and National Insurance contributions, it will barely be enough to buy food never mind put a roof over your head or create the lifestyle you've been dreaming of since you started work all those years ago.

Hey, I'm planning on a retirement full of cruises round the Med and hot and cold running toyboys. I'm not going to get that on the state pension so I certainly need to put a bit more aside elsewhere.

So, if, like me, you would like a little more than the absolute basics to live on you need to:

- *Make sure you are getting all the money you can from the state.*
- *Make sure you are getting best value from any company pension entitlements (see page 134).*
- *Create the best type of personal pension for your circumstances, if you need one (see page 139).*
- *Start thinking about an annuity when you are close to retirement (see page 148).*
- *Dream about and plan what you'd love to do when you've retired.*

This last point, dreaming about what you'd like to do, goes to the heart of my thinking on pretty much everything – financial or not. The whole point of being here is to enjoy a good life. To do that you have to know what a 'good life' for you would look like.

Do you want to travel, pursue a hobby, start a business, collect bottle tops, learn Japanese, help out at the local children's hospice, become an extreme knitter? Go back to your list of goals (the one mentioned on page 41) and think again about how much you will need.

The government's own website has some suggestions and some points to be aware of as you approach retirement. Go to Direct.gov.uk then click on the orange heading 'Pensions and Retirement Planning' then click on the 'Guide to planning for retirement'.

Now that you've worked out what it is you want to do when you're retired we now have to set about making sure you have enough money coming in to be able to do it!

# First Thing: Get Everything You Can From the State

## STATE PENSION

The full state pension is currently, wait for it, £95.25 a week for a single person or £152.30 for a couple. Even if you are reading this book in 2020 it won't be much better – it may even be worse. Give it another 20 or 30 years and who knows what, if anything, will be provided. Seriously.

The figures above tell us two things about the state pension:

- *It's not enough.*
- *The government seems to want us to get divorced before we claim a pension.*

It doesn't matter which political party is in power, the government cannot afford to pay you and me enough of a pension to live off right now. What's more, with all the debt that our beloved leaders have taken on in the last few years, pension payments from the state are only going to get worse.

You may not even qualify for the full state pension. It will depend upon:

- *Your age*
- *How many years you have paid National Insurance contributions*

If you were born on or before 5 April 1950 you may (note only 'may') be entitled to a state pension from the age of 60 for women and 65 for men. Women born after that will have to wait until they are 65 or older, and men can look forward to waiting until they are 68 or older if they are intending to claim their pension after 2024.

Once you reach that age you will be entitled to the state pension if you have paid National Insurance contributions for a sufficient number of years – these are called qualifying years. For men it's currently 44, for women 39 – though this number drops to 30 if you hit state pension age after 6 April 2010.

If you've been receiving certain benefits (e.g. Carer's, Jobseeker's, Incapacity, Employment and Support) you may have received National Insurance credits. You can check this by getting in touch with your local tax office. You can either phone the number on correspondence you've had from the tax office or phone the helpline on the HMRC website: hmrc.gov.uk.

## GET A STATE PENSION FORECAST

There are lots of variables that will affect what you are entitled to, so there is a government-run 'State Pensions Forecast Team' that you can contact:

> Future Pension Centre
> Tyneview Park
> Whitley Road
> Newcastle upon Tyne
> NE98 1BA
> 0845 3000 168

You will have to complete some forms and they will then send you your forecast. This forecast will tell you what state pension-related benefits you are set to receive including:

- *The state pension*
- *The second state pension (see below)*
- *The over 80 pension (a means-tested pension for people over 80 who don't qualify for a state pension)*
- *Extra benefits for dependants*
- *How you might be able to improve your state pension*
- *The effect on your second state pension if you are 'contracted out'*

## SECOND STATE PENSION (S2P)

This replaced SERPS (State Earnings-Related Pension Scheme) with the intention of giving a more generous additional state pension to low earners, certain carers and people with long-term illness or disability.

By around 2030 the S2P will become a simple, flat-rate weekly top-up to the basic state pension – i.e. not much. When you claim your state pension any additional state pension will be added automatically. If you want to take the money out of your S2P in order to put it in a pension provider that you think will perform better for you then you need to make sure you understand the implications of 'contracting out' (see below).

For more information on all things state pension related go to the excellent government-funded websites:

- *Direct.gov.uk: click on 'Pensions and Retirement Planning'*
- *Pensionsadvisoryservice.org.uk*

### CONTRACTING OUT – MOVING YOUR PENSION OUT OF THE SECOND STATE PENSION (S2P)

If you are entitled to an S2P then the government will have a pot of cash that is allocated to you from which you will receive an S2P. If you reckon you would get a higher payment from this pot of cash by putting it into another pension then you can contract out of the S2P.

There are restrictions on who can contract out depending upon their circumstances. Should you contract out and then want to contract back in again there will be various implications on government contributions to your S2P and the National Insurance payments that you and your employer will have paid. There are also restrictions on who can contract back in.

These and many, many more details including how to actually go about contracting out (and back in (and shaking it all about)) are covered in the free guide you can download from the FSA site, MoneyMadeClear, specifically www.money madeclear.fsa.gov.uk/pdfs/contracting_out.pdf. Alternatively you can call them on 0845 60 60 265.

# Get Everything You are Entitled to from Your Company Pension(s)

The state will, at best, provide you with a few hundred pounds a month . . . before tax! Yep, all the payments you receive from your pension(s) are subject to tax.

So the next stone to look under is company pensions. Having a company pension does not affect your S2P entitlements.

Most companies are obliged to offer their employees the opportunity to join a company pension. However, this may simply be their showing you a stakeholder pension that they will automatically make payments into from your salary before tax, but they won't add in anything extra themselves.

If your company does offer a pension then it's worth looking into for two reasons:

- *The company might offer to contribute to your pension.*
- *The money is taken out of your gross salary, i.e. before tax. That's a useful little discipline that means money is going into your*

*pension without you feeling it or having to make it happen. Essentially, you're protecting your future self from your current, spending self!*

There are two types of company pension: Final Salary and Money Purchase.

Final Salary, or Defined Benefit, schemes provide a guaranteed pension payment to the pension holder (you and me) – e.g. once retired you would definitely receive, say, £1,000 a month no matter how badly the economy and stock market had performed up to the point at which you start claiming your pension.

These have all but disappeared because they place a massively expensive and unpredictable burden on the pension provider – be it your employer or the pension company that is providing the programme for your company. The reason for this is that the pension provider takes your money and invests it (usually quite badly) in stock markets and whatnot. If these investments perform badly then they have lost money but they still have to keep their promise of paying you £1,000 a month once you've retired.

This is exactly what has happened with pensions over the last 20 years. So if your company does provide a Defined Benefit/Final Salary scheme then, assuming it does pay a good final benefit, it will be hard to beat.

Unsurprisingly the pension companies decided that their having to be responsible for their own cock-ups wasn't fair. So they very helpfully came up with Money Purchase or Defined Contribution schemes.

As you've probably already worked out, these are schemes in which the only fixed amount of money changing hands is what you give them each month towards your pension investment. What you get when you retire depends on how well/badly they've invested your money.

So the value of such a pension very much depends upon whether or not your employer contributes. The likely decisions you need to consider are shown in the box below:

| Your situation | What you should consider |
|---|---|
| Your employer offers a Final Salary/ Defined Benefit pension | Look at the amount you are guaranteed to receive in pension payments. If this is any good (in other words, it's going to be enough to live on comfortably when you retire) then this pension will definitely be worth joining or maintaining. |
| Your employer offers a Money Purchase/ Defined Contribution AND contributes to your pension | This is worthy of serious consideration, but find out if your employer would be prepared to contribute the same amount to an alternative pension in your name. If they would then you need to investigate alternative pension options (see personal pensions) as this will give you a 'mobile' pension i.e. if you want to leave that company then you don't have to worry about setting up a new pension. If you do move your money out of the company pension then you also need to be aware of the implications of contracting out (see page 133). |
| Your employer makes a Money Purchase/ Defined Contribution scheme available to you BUT makes no contribution to it | Have a look at the pension they are offering, find out everything you can about it and then compare that to the alternative pensions available to you. The latter could well offer you greater control, flexibility and return. Once again be aware of the implications of contracting out. |
| Your employer does not make any pension available to you at all. | They may be breaking the law if they employ at least five people and you earn more than £95 per week (for tax year ending April 2010). If you're not sure check with the Pensions Regulator (see contact details on page 157). Either way you need to be thinking very seriously about setting up your own personal pension as soon as possible. |

## PAYING EXTRA INTO A GOOD COMPANY PENSION

If you have decided that your company pension is very good (i.e. you can see what the pension provider is investing in and it looks good) then you might wish to increase your contributions to the pension.

Another reason to increase your contributions could be that you have worked out what your combined total pension is likely to be and it has frightened the life out of you because it's so low and you want to boost it pronto.

### WANT TO FIND OUT WHAT TOTAL PENSION YOU WILL GET?

The Combined Pensions Forecast team used to provide this service but it has vanished as far as consumers are concerned.

All is not lost, though: you can contact the Future Pension Centre (see page 132) for your state pension, your employer for your company pension and your own personal pension provider for your own personal pension if you have one. Combine all three pensions (i.e. add up the monthly pension payment you'll receive on retirement that each one forecasts) and you have your answer.

Alternatively phone the Pensions Advisory Service on 0845 601 2923, email them at enquiries@pensionsadvisoryservice. org.uk or join in on one of their live online Q&As where you can ask all sorts of pensiony questions!

As with everything else concerning pensions, you have to use yet another three-letter abbreviation if you want to increase the amount you pay into your pension. This exciting abbreviation is AVC – Additional Voluntary Contributions (never let it be said that the financial community contains more than its fair share of BS).

Anyway, thanks to the pension regulations amendments made in 2006 you are now allowed to save more or less as much as you like into any number and type of pensions up to a total of £1.5 million overall. Keep in mind, though, that there is an 'annual allowance' which limits you to putting in up to £255,000 per tax year (although that limit could change in the future so keep an eye on the HMRC website).You can do this no matter how young you are (ahem!) and you'll get tax relief as outlined on page 147.

## WHAT DO YOU DO NEXT?

So you've discovered that your state pension is going to be pitiful. You've checked your company pension situation and worked out that one of the following most closely matches your situation:

A.  When added to your state pension you are going to be rolling in cash when you hit retirement – bring it on!
B.  You reckon your company pension is not very good and you want to put that investment into a different pension that will perform better.
C.  Your combined pension forecast is just not good enough. You are going to have to set up a personal pension to make sure you have enough when you are retired/over 55.
D.  You are self-employed and don't have access to any company pension whether good, bad or just plain mediocre.

If you are in category A, then well done! Make sure you have read the other chapters of this book, then hurry off to the nearest tea and cake stall to celebrate.

Those of you in categories B, C and D need to read the following section on 'Personal Pensions' very closely.

# Personal Pensions

We've reached the point now where it's crucial to understand what a 'pension' really is: a source of passive income that will more than pay your bills when you are not in a position to do so yourself.

There are some key characteristics that make pensions different from most other forms of investment:

- *The earliest you are allowed to draw funds from a pension is when you hit 55.*
- *The money that you put into a pension gets attractive tax benefits (see tax relief on pensions on page 147).*
- *It's almost always set up with the long term in mind.*

So within those parameters, it's an investment with all the same challenges of any other investment. Therefore when selecting what pension investment is best, the questions to ask yourself once again revolve around these:

- *How much money can you afford to invest?*
- *Do you want something that is actively managed but expensive?*
- *What level of risk and consequent likely reward fits your portfolio?*
- *How active do you want to be in the management of the investment?*

There are three main types of pension to which I'll be applying those questions:

- *Stakeholder*
- *Standard*
- *SIPP (Self-Invested Personal Pension)*

# Stakeholder Pensions

*Investment level: beginner*

These are the low-effort, low-cost, transparent option. Payments into a stakeholder pension can be as low as £20 a month so they're affordable for everyone (the pension provider is obliged to accept payments this small). The maximum the provider can charge a year is 1.5% of the total value of the pension and they're not allowed to charge you for transferring money into or out of the stakeholder pension. As you may have guessed, the government created legislation for these pensions to stop pensions companies from making all sorts of excessive charges and also to make the whole pension process a bit more transparent. I'd say those aims have been achieved. Many companies, rather than offering a company pension, point their staff at a stakeholder pension as it's much cheaper and easier than going through the rigmarole of setting one up themselves.

My thinking is that, if you want a personal pension, it's probably worth setting up a stakeholder even if it's just to put £20 a month in. Should your company be prepared to contribute to this pension as well then it's a very attractive option indeed.

And while you're at it, set one up for your kids, spouse and anyone else you love enough to stretch the budget to. That's how much I like them!

## SELECTING A STAKEHOLDER PENSION

You can compare stakeholder pensions at the website of the Financial Services Authority – www.fsa.gov.uk/tables/bespoke/Pensions. Pensions advisers can help you compare stakeholder schemes with the benefit of expert advice, although they will have to be paid for their advice – whether it's commission (not great) or a fee for their time (much better). See Appendix 2 for advice on how to pick a good financial adviser.

Be prepared, as always, to research the options yourself. You can do most of this on Moneymagpie.com, of course, and on money websites like ThisIsMoney.co.uk and Fool.co.uk. Also, keep an eye on coverage in the financial sections of national 'broadsheet' newspapers.

To compare charges and fund choice within stakeholder pensions (but not past performance), visit www.fsa.gov.uk/tables/bespoke/Pensions.

Because of the low charges that are imposed on these products, many stakeholder pension funds are set up as tracker funds. This is because trackers (as you have seen in Chapter 4) are run by computers and, therefore, charge low annual fees. As I've stated throughout the book, I'm a big fan of tracker funds – they are cheap and give a pretty good return. See page 99 in Chapter 4 for a full explanation of tracker funds and how they work.

# Standard Personal Pensions

*Investment level: avoid*

Before the introduction of stakeholder pensions in 2000 and even before the introduction of SIPPs (see opposite), the only kind of personal pension you could get was one that was managed by fund managers within a pension company. You can still get these, and some of them perform fairly well but most of them don't. This is because these are just managed funds placed within the parameters of a pension. As I've outlined on page 120 in Chapter 4, I don't like most managed funds because they are expensive (in other words they have high annual fees) and the majority of them do pretty poorly.

I dislike standard pensions for all the same reasons that, conversely, I like stakeholder pensions: like managed investment funds, standard personal pensions are expensive, inflexible, usually grossly overpriced and, all too often, badly managed. Stakeholder pensions, on the other hand, are cheap and you have a pretty clear idea of what they're investing in.

So if you are not already in one then my preference would be to stay out!

If you find you are in one then you need to start asking questions of the pension provider to determine how bad the charges and fees will be for taking money out. If the fees are abominably high then you may well be better off leaving your money in there and freezing it (i.e. keeping it as it is and not adding any more to it) while, at the same time, setting up a new stakeholder or SIPP to run alongside it.

If you find that the withdrawal charges aren't too bad and you have spent time researching and taking advice to find a better pension home for that money then you can start the painful process of taking your money out of the standard pension. Believe me, they will make it as difficult and tedious as legally possible for you to take your money out. You'll receive form after form to fill in by hand that you'll have to post back then hassle them to do anything. It will take weeks so be prepared.

Why are they so unhappy about you taking your money out? Because there is no limit to the fees (the annual service charge if you like) that they can charge you in a standard personal pension. That's all you need to know. (You may, at this point, wish to come up with some three-letter abbreviations for the people behind these pensions!)

> **What they want you to do:** put money into whichever high-charging personal pension they're currently peddling.
> **What you should do:** consider a stakeholder and/or a SIPP to give yourself a low-cost, decent investment product.

# SIPPs

*Investment level: all levels*

You can tell it's getting exciting now – the abbreviations are up to four letters. Do self-invested personal pensions deserve this level of euphoria? If you are prepared to put in the time and effort, and you have at least £25,000 (better still £50,000) to invest in them, then the answer is probably 'yes'. If you have a smaller amount than that then the costs will probably render it too expensive compared to a stakeholder pension.

A SIPP is a kind of pensions 'bag'. Into this bag you can put a broad range of investments that you choose and once they're in the SIPP they have all the tax benefits and access regulations that all pensions have. You can include in your SIPP: equities, cash deposits, futures, commercial property, unit and investment trusts among other asset classes. The pension world is your oyster.

Where do you start? Well, imagine you are investing in shares or bonds but were able to wrap them in a tax-proof blanket BUT you can't touch them until you are at least 55. That's more or less the opportunity and challenge that a SIPP presents.

So let's start at the low-effort, low-sophistication end of the scale and work our way up.

## LOW-COST PROVIDERS

*Investment level: beginner to intermediate*

One of the pleasant knock-on effects of stakeholder pensions is that the costs for pension provision have been forced down elsewhere. Low-cost, usually online, providers are a case in point.

Low-cost or 'supermarket' SIPPs offer a selection of funds, stocks and other investments for you to choose from within the confines of your SIPP.

Yes, you have to do the selecting, so it's time to study those funds, shares, stocks, bonds and whatnot. Alternatively you could keep it fairly simple and dependable and pick tracker funds that are on a fairly reliable wicket (see pages 99–104 for more about trackers and why I like them).

This is quite possibly one of my all-time favourite invest-ment combinations:

- *Low-cost SIPP provider*
- *Low-cost but dependable tracker fund*
- *Tax relief on the whole thing*

Competitive providers include Hargreaves Lansdowne (Hargreaveslansdown.com), Fidelity FundsNetwork (Fidelity.co.uk), James Hay (Jameshay.co.uk) and Killik (Killik.com).

## INSURANCE SIPPs

*Investment level: intermediate*

Once again we are in the realm of paying for investment advice as part of the service here and, as you may have gathered by now, I am of the opinion that the advice for which you are paying is often so bad that they should be paying you compen-sation for messing up your investment (and are sometimes forced to, though not enough I think).

Having seen the joys of cheap, simple stakeholder pensions and low-cost SIPPs the insurance (also known as deferred or hybrid) SIPPs look like an option that I personally would avoid.

They work by providing the whole fund put in place for you, or a selection of managed funds to choose from. It's fairly effortless for you but no less effort than selecting a simple stakeholder pension containing tracker funds.

## FULL SIPPs

*Investment level: advanced*

These are high risk, high effort, large investment required, but the highest potential return.

Take everything from the section on stock-picking on page 113 and come back to apply it here. It's all up to you so you'd better be prepared to do the necessary research.

You might expect these SIPPs to be low cost because you are putting in all the effort, but they may not necessarily be because the full SIPP providers will charge you for every trade you make – they may even charge you for 'inactivity'!

If you are feeling up to the challenge of managing your own fund then, according to Robbie Burns in *The Naked Trader*, who 'loves' his full SIPP, you'll need two things:

- *An execution-only stockbroker (online ones are cheapest)*
- *A pension trustee*

The trustee looks after your money, keeping it secure in a recognised pension account (i.e. you can't dip into it before you are 55) for an annual fee of around £150 to £300. When you pay however much of your salary you want into your full SIPP the tax rebate (20%, 40%, 50% depending upon your tax bracket) will be added automatically.

I've listed execution-only online brokers to consider on page 317. It might be best to start with a broker you like and then see if they have any special deals with good pension trustees.

If you are going to go down this route then remember, you are looking for long-term growth and this is money that you are going to really need when the time comes around. So keep the risk level low to moderate.

## TAX RELIEF AND CONTRIBUTION LEVELS

Contribution level: You can contribute up to 100% of your salary (with a ceiling of £245,000) a year in any number and type of pensions. You pay 40% on any contributions above that amount.

Tax relief: Tax relief is paid on contributions you make to your pension according to your tax bracket. If your salary is taxed at 20% then for every £80 you put into a pension a further £20 will be added by the government (or the full £100 will be placed straight into the company pension by your employer before tax is charged against it).

Capital gains tax: The pension fund is not subject to capital gains tax. So if it grows in value then the pension keeps all of that growth – it's protected from the taxman.

Tax-free lump sum: When you retire you can take up to 25% of the value of your personal pensions savings as a tax-free lump sum. There is a ceiling of 25% on the 'lifetime allowance' for the year in which you take this lump sum. For 2010–11 the lifetime allowance is £1.8 million; 25% of that is £450,000. So it's a pretty high ceiling!

If you take more than 25% of your total pension savings then you will be charged 25% on the excess (55% if you are exceeding 25% of the lifetime allowance).

Non-taxpayers: Non-taxpayers can get tax relief of 20% on pensions contributions up to £2,880 a year. So if you put £2,880 in, the government will top it up to £3,600.

Paying into someone else's pension: If you pay into someone else's pension fund then, as with non-taxpayers, the tax relief is 20% up to £2,880.

## Annuities – Have Cash Coming in After You Retire

(NB You can skip this bit if you're not retiring for at least another five years)

Annuities are guaranteed income for the rest of your life (or for a fixed period of time – you can get temporary annuities as well). You hand over a lump sum (at least £5,000) and you receive a guaranteed amount of money every year. Basically, it's an industry word for your pension!

The average rate of return for annuities is around 5–6% annually but, not surprisingly, the amount you get, per £1,000 of your money, depends on how long the annuity company guesses you will live. So the rate you are quoted will depend on how old you are when you start your annuity, what gender you are (women tend to live longer than men) and how healthy you seem (smokers and obese people, for example, are not expected to live as long as those who lead a healthy lifestyle).

The most important thing to remember with annuities is that you should shop around for the best rate you can find. For far too long, pensioners have simply accepted the annuity that their pension company has offered, assuming that that was the only one they had access to and not realising that it's an open market and they could perhaps get a better rate elsewhere (in fact, they probably would). So make sure that you contact various pension companies to see which would offer you the most cash.

The other point to consider is that the money you get each year is fixed so over time the value of your annual income will be eroded by inflation. So, for example, you might have the money to go out for dinner once a week at £20 a time right now but when you come to retire that same meal could cost you closer to £40 so you need to make sure that you will have a higher income to be able to afford the lifestyle you have right now. Again, the way to combat this is to go for an index-linked product – that means a product that guarantees you an income that goes up and down with the rate of inflation. However, this does mean that you lose a lot in the first few years. For example, in 2009, a 65-year-old man could expect an income of between £564–£632 per month for every £10,000 invested in an annuity. However, if he went for an index-linked one he would only get just over £300 a month. So it's quite a question you need to ask yourself: how long are you planning on living? If you are planning on hanging around for a good long time (and I hope you are!) then it's worth seriously considering the index-linked version. If you don't expect to have too many years to come then the basic annuity would be best. It's a nasty choice to make.

Unless you have gone for a temporary policy, there's no way you can get your hands on the capital and use it to invest in something else. Once it's done, it's done, so make sure you go for a good one!

If you have invested in a pension then (as you can see below) some (though not all) of your money has to be invested in an annuity. However, the rest of it, and any other money you have when you retire, doesn't have to be put into an annuity. You could put all or some of it into a savings account, gilts or bonds (see Chapter 6 for information on those).

The advantage of annuities is that the amount you get each year is guaranteed for the rest of your life. The disadvantage is that you might be able to get better rates later on elsewhere. No one has a crystal ball, so my advice would be to put some of your money into an annuity and spread the rest around the best savings rates and gilts rates you can find, keeping in mind that these can change over the years. In other words you could win or lose whatever you do, so it's best to do a mix!

## PURCHASED AND COMPULSORY ANNUITIES

*Investing level: medium to advanced*
*Safety level: high*

Annuities generally fall into one of two broad categories: compulsory purchase annuities, or simply 'pension annuities', and purchased life annuities, which are also known as 'immediate life annuities'.

Compulsory purchase annuities are retirement financial plans that ensure you receive a fixed income until you die, payable monthly, quarterly, half yearly or annually and funded by a pension plan you hold. If you hold an occupational pension, the company you work for will organise an annuity for you upon your retirement and this is done automatically. If you hold a personal pension, your provider will present you with their annuity offerings but unlike occupational pensions, you are under no obligation to accept it, and shopping around for an 'open market option' in order to get the best deal is definitely my advice – you could substantially boost your income if you do. As the name suggests, it's compulsory by law to buy an annuity if you have a pension, although you are allowed to take a 25% tax-free lump sum from your pension before doing so. You can't buy an annuity before the age of 55, and you must have one arranged by the age of 75 unless you opt for an alternatively secured pension (ASP).

Purchased life annuities are annuities bought with money other than that in your pension fund, whether it be from an investment, an inheritance, the proceeds from an ISA or any other lump sum.

One of the advantages of purchased life annuities (not with compulsory life annuities, though) is that not all of your income is taxed. Some of it is classed as a return of your capital and you are deemed to have paid tax on this already (you're effectively just being given back your own money in bits) so that part of the income isn't taxed, although the rest (considered interest on the capital) is taxed. Because of this, the quotes you receive for these from providers will differ from that of compulsory annuities.

Under these two umbrella terms, there are a whole host of annuities on the market, all of which serve different purposes and have their own perks and drawbacks. Here are just a few that are available:

## With-profits annuities/unit-linked annuities

These are two different products which are similar in nature. With with-profits, your income essentially has two levels: a guaranteed minimum sum that is fixed, and bonuses that come as a result of investment in a with-profits fund. Your income is partially protected by 'smoothing', which refers to the practice of withholding bonuses in years where investments have yielded, to cover possible future losses. Unit-linked annuities are similar but there is no income security and the ante is upped with regards to risk, as your income is more directly tied up in the investments that underpin your policy.

With both, your income is based on an anticipated bonus rate, chosen by you when opening the annuity, and this figure is usually between 0% and 5%. If you go for a fund with a medium-risk 2% rate and the insurance company announces a 3% bonus rate at the end of the year, your income will rise accordingly. If the company announces a 1% bonus, your rate will fall in line with this. The volatility of bonuses is higher with unit-linked funds.

The composition of the funds will differ with each provider; the majority of the investments will go into equities, but the proportions will be more varied across bonds, property and cash according to the provider.

See my notes in Chapter 10 about with-profits and unit-linked products. I'm not keen on these products – sometimes they work but much of the time they involve too many charges and, frankly, too much messing about by fund managers who aren't as good as they should be.

## Enhanced pension annuities

These are for people who do not have a clean bill of health, including anything from diabetes and arthritis to being a heavy smoker; with Hargreaves & Lansdown, there are over 1,500 conditions that would drive your annuity income up! This is because life assurance companies take the view that you are more likely to die sooner rather than later (vultures!) if you have a chequered medical history, and will therefore be prepared to pay you a better income.

For all intents and purposes, you are entering into a 'bet' with the life assurance company that you will live for a long time, with your 'stake' being the premium you pay. It is largely informed guesswork on the part of the life assurers. When you go for a quote for an annuity, you are first asked a whole bunch of questions by the provider over the phone. The information you provide them (about your health, your pension scheme, and even your postcode) will be inputted into a snazzy piece of software, nondescript calculations are made and an estimated time of death is churned out.

From this, they can work out how much they can pay you up until that point so you receive an income akin to your initial investment. If you live to be 110, the life assurance company 'lose' as they will have to continue paying you the agreed income long after your initial investment has been used. If you drop down dead the day after taking out the annuity, the life company will pocket the cash and 'win', if you like (unless, of course, you have guaranteed your annuity – see below). It's by no means an exact science, and risk assessment is at the heart of it, as with most financial products.

Aside from the different types of annuity, there is also a whole host of glamorous (not) 'bolt-ons' available that allow you to tailor your plan, all of which will have some effect on the income you receive:

### Guarantee periods

These do what they say on the tin and guarantee your income for a set period. Should you guarantee your annuity for 10 years and die after three, your estate will continue to receive the due payments for the remaining seven years. If you don't guarantee your plan, it will cease when you die.

### Single/joint life options

A single life option provides income for the holder of the policy only until death. A joint life option pays an income to the holder and a beneficiary (such as a spouse) until both parties have died.

### Level/escalating income

You can choose to fix the level of income you receive over the term of your annuity, or you can choose to have it increase over time, either by a fixed percentage each year or in line with inflation. Of course, if you opt for the latter your early payments will be smaller, to account for increasing payments later on. On the other hand, inflation could significantly eat into your fixed income as years pass by, so you will need to assess whether you intend to stick around long enough to benefit from an escalating income.

### Value protection

This is essentially another type of guarantee stipulating that if you were to die before the age of 75, a beneficiary would receive all (full protection) or some (partial protection) of the sum paid for the annuity (minus the income already paid), subject to tax at 35%.

The most important thing to remember with any form of annuity is that you need to shop around and do a lot of research before you leap in and buy one. Whichever pension company you have been contributing to over the years will contact you directly and persuasively as you come to the time when you could take out an annuity. They will do their best to get you to take their low-rate annuity and sign on the dotted line as soon as they can. Don't bow to their persuasion.

You have the whole of the annuity market to choose from and rates can vary wildly from company to company. The difference between the best and worst annuities can be as much as 25% so it's always worth shopping around.

## HOW TO INVEST IN THESE

It's first worth finding out which ones are on the market, and these can be found by – yep, you guessed it – online search engines and comparison sites.

The Financial Services Authority (www.fsa.gov.uk/tables) has a handy website which makes the whole subject a little more digestible, and allows you to rifle through the annuities on offer and get quotes based on a small questionnaire you fill out detailing your circumstances. Hargreaves Lansdown also has an annuity service (www.h-l.co.uk/pensions/Annuities) which searches a large number of providers for you to find you a competitive rate, and Beatthatquote.com is yet another resource which allows you to compare providers.

Once again, it is important that you have gone round the houses and are sure about what it is you're getting yourself into because there's no opting out once papers have been signed and those cheques start coming through. Here's what to do:

- *Get a quote from your current pension company (this is not applicable if you aren't paying for the annuity with your pension fund).*
- *Think about what you want to do in retirement, and whether you have anyone you need to provide for, e.g. young children. Also consider some of the above bolt-ons, and assess whether you would be better off integrating some of them into your plan.*
- *If you think there is some money of yours gathering dust in a pension scheme you joined at an old job, you may be able to locate it through the Pensions Tracing Service (go to Direct.gov.uk for a link to it). By providing information about the company that you worked for, you can claim what is rightfully yours and boost your income.*
- *Contact the DWP (Department of Work and Pensions) at Dwp.gov.uk and request an estimate of the state pension you will receive.*
- *Contact the providers outlining what it is you want from your annuity and ask for a competitive quote!*

## GENERAL PENSION CONTACT DETAILS

Government website

www.direct.gov.uk/en/Pensionsandretirementplanning/index.htm

There is a load of info here: videos, guides, articles and more.

Pensions Advisory Service

0845 601 2923

www.pensionsadvisoryservice.org.uk/

enquiries@pensionsadvisoryservice.org.uk

The Pensions Regulator

Napier House

Trafalgar Place

Brighton

BN1 4DW

0870 606 3636

customersupport@thepensionsregulator.gov.uk

www.thepensionsregulator.gov.uk

Money Made Clear – the FSA website

0300 500 5000

www.moneymadeclear.fsa.gov.uk/hubs/home_pensions.html

Pensions have had a bad rap in recent years, and understandably, but I recommend that you have at least a small amount of money invested in one, as well as all your other investments. It's particularly handy from a tax point of view (especially if you are on the higher rate) and it's an important element of spreading your money across different products. Speaking of which – let's have a look at bonds next.

## Chapter 6

# Bonds – The Security Holding Your Investments Together

Do your eyes glaze over when you see the word 'bonds' in the newspaper?

Do you look blankly at the page when it mentions 'gilts'?

I don't blame you. I've done the same. Actually, though, they're not that hard to grasp once you know the basic facts about them.

Bonds are less risky than shares, on the whole, but generally more risky than cash investments (unless your cash is with an Icelandic bank, but that's another story). They've become a lot more popular in recent years although most people still don't really understand what they are or how they work.

If you have already invested in a pension and some shares you should consider diversifying into bonds too. If you don't mind making a portion of your money inaccessible for a fixed period, you could benefit from better rates by opting for bonds.

Also, the longer you are willing to keep your cash out of reach and the more you deposit, the higher the interest will be.

## Bonds – No, Not That Type of Bond . . .

'Bond' is possibly one of the most annoying and confusing words in the world of finance. It's used for so many different things you really have to check and re-check to make sure you're putting your money in the right thing.

Somehow, marketing departments have decided that the word 'bond' has a nice, posh, trustworthy sound to it – more appealing than 'fixed-rate' or 'we want your cash' – so they insist on using it wherever possible. In Chapter 3 I covered 'savings bonds', which is just another term for fixed-rate savings accounts where you put your money in at a certain rate for a certain length of time and that's it. Also in this book you will hear of structured, life insurance-based products that have the word 'bond' in them – again, I think, simply because it's a nice, trustworthy-sounding word. Precipice bonds and with-profits bonds are about as profitable as, though less useful than, Brooke Bonds, Basildon Bonds and James Bonds.

You just have to swallow your annoyance, I'm afraid, and keep a clear head, as always, when reading literature which mentions the word 'bond' in any context.

## . . . This Type of Bond

Proper bonds – those that, in my opinion, really have a right to the name – are loans made either to governments or to companies. Whereas with shares you actually own some of a company – well, you don't exactly own a piece of it, rather you own the rights to some of the profits of it and some of its growth – with bonds you don't own anything tangible. You are just lending and benefiting (you hope) from the interest (also called the 'coupon') they pay on that loan and, at the end of the term, from the amount that bond has grown in value (again, you hope).

Organisations issue bonds because, for example, a company needs to build a new office building, or needs to buy new equipment, or expand. Or maybe a government needs to improve the infrastructure of the country or set up a new department. Whatever the need, a large sum of money will be needed to get the job done.

So they issue (sell) a bond. A bond is an IOU issued by a company or the government in return for it borrowing some money. The IOU states that the holder of the bond will be paid back a fixed sum of money (e.g. £100) after a fixed period of time (e.g. five years).

During this period of time the issuer of the bond (the company or the government) will give you an interest payment on the money you've lent them – usually the interest is paid every six months. A bond issued by the government is very safe – so safe that it's referred to as 'gilt edged' or simply, a gilt.

## TAX AND BONDS

One rather good reason for investing in bonds is the tax advantage they have over shares and savings accounts.

You will have to pay income tax on the interest on gilts, corporate bonds and PIBs although it is usually paid out without any income tax being deducted, unlike savings accounts for example. Also, you can put gilts, corporate bonds and PIBs into an ISA and therefore avoid paying any income tax on them.

Any capital gains you make on gilts are free from tax (although this is not the case with corporate bonds and PIBs). So say you buy a gilt with a price of £80 and a redemption value of £100. If you hold the gilt until redemption, the gain of £20 would be tax free. However, you don't get any relief for capital losses. So if you bought a gilt for £120 that had a redemption value of £100 you would not be able to offset the loss of £20 against any other gains you made.

Unlike shares, you don't have to pay any stamp duty when you buy gilts, corporate bonds or PIBs. This is important because one of the problems that individuals and, in particular, pension funds have had in the last few years is that the dividend tax rebate was removed from equity investments. So if you see a share yielding 5% and a bond yielding 5%, the yield on the share in your ISA would be 1/9th less than for the bond. Interesting, huh?

# Why Invest in Bonds?

There are a few reasons why you might like to invest in different types of bonds at different stages of your investing career.

# DIVERSIFICATION

Yes, it's that word again. But it's true. Bonds are one of the four main asset classes (the others are cash, shares and property) and bonds/gilts often do well when others are doing badly.

Generally speaking bonds offer a steady and predictable return and in most cases you are almost certain to get your whole investment back as well as the interest payments. (The big exception to this being junk bonds – see below.)

Many people believe it makes sense to invest a proportion of your portfolio in bonds to provide some protection against the volatility of shares. One rule of thumb that is quoted on a regular basis is that an individual should have the same percentage of their portfolio invested in bonds as their age. So a 40-year-old should have 40% in bonds, a 50-year-old 50% and so on. Such guidelines are crude at best, though, as they don't account for an individual's attitude to risk. For example, if you are a 50-year-old with a large portfolio or one who is happy to take risks then you might want to put a lower proportion than 50% of your investment portfolio into bonds.

# SECURITY

As you will see from the separate box overleaf, 'risk and reward' bonds can offer extremely safe and predictable investment options.

By setting aside a portion of your investment portfolio with gilts or investment-grade bonds you are able to create a bedrock of safe money that provides a small, reliable return. This frees you up to be a little more adventurous with other parts of the portfolio.

## INCOME

The income generated by bonds can be used in an even more specific way. If you are nearing or past retirement age and want to have money coming in from your investments in a predictable, reliable series of payments that you can live off then gilts or very safe corporate bonds are a favourite investment.

## GROWTH

The growth potential of bonds applies mostly to junk bonds. If you can afford to risk money on a number of them then there is a chance that one of them might have been issued by a company that has a staggering turnaround rendering the bonds far more valuable. The more likely scenario is that the bonds will default and you'll lose your money. Gilts and investment-grade bonds offer safe, predictable returns so their value probably won't change much.

## RISK AND REWARD

As with so much in the world of investing, the whole 'risk and reward' principle very much applies to bonds. If you have ever tried to borrow yourself you will have noticed that lenders will first try and calculate whether you're good for the loan or a bit of a dodgy customer. If they think they have a good chance of getting their money back from you they will offer you a nice low interest rate. However, if they think you could potentially default they will cover themselves by insisting on a high interest rate so that they can rake in a goodly wodge of cash early on before you do the dirty on them.

It's the same in reverse when you invest in bonds (loans). Different companies and governments have different 'credit ratings' depending on how secure the ratings agencies (Moody's and Standard & Poor are the main ones) consider them to be. A big solid company like Microsoft or Mobil will have top security ratings, AAA in fact (although even with dependable companies such as these, AAA ratings are few and far between). Nice safe European governments will have top ratings too. This is because with these organisations you have more than a fighting chance of getting your money back and more. It's still a chance, though, and there is certainly risk involved. However, because the risk is low the return is also comparatively low, particularly with loans to governments.

Smaller more volatile companies, and countries with 1,000% inflation would have much lower credit ratings and, therefore, offer higher interest rates for your loan.

That all makes sense (I hope) except that the system is by no means foolproof, as the collapse of Enron (given 'investment' grade at the time) showed in 2002. Even worse was the 2007–9 crisis when these big and important ratings agencies gave AAA ratings to huge investment products that were based purely on sub-prime home loans which then imploded spectacularly. Suddenly the ratings agencies had egg on their faces and their judgements on companies, and on investment products particularly, were definitely under question, and still are.

Many times, bonds will be secured against the assets of the company so even if they go bust the bond holders may get something. Or a company may fall on hard times and while the equity could fall completely, the bond holders would usually be kept whole. If you can't imagine a company going bust but could imagine the management getting things very badly wrong, then bonds make sense. If you're pretty certain that it will one day be taken over and are reasonably sure that it will happen soon then maybe buy their shares. If you have no idea but you can't imagine the UK high street with loads of empty space then buy their bonds.

So, as with everything, when it comes to investing in bonds, even in gilts, it's 'buyer beware'!

## Which Type of Bond is Right for You?

Different bonds work for different people. Also, you might be at a stage where you would like a mix of different bonds, from no risk to lots of risk, in your portfolio. Which ones (and what percentage of them) you go for depends on your situation. Here are some suggestions:

### YOU WOULD LIKE A NICE, SAFE, REGULAR INCOME THAT YOU DON'T HAVE TO WORRY ABOUT:

#### Gilts or government bonds are the ones to go for

They're dull, but safe. Also, as mentioned above, if economic times are tough and turbulent you can find that your pedestrian gilts are outperforming all the other major asset classes, which will make you smile (see page 163 for more information).

## YOU WOULD PREFER A MEDIUM-RISK, SLIGHTLY HIGHER RETURN TO UNDERPIN THE REST OF YOUR PORTFOLIO:

### Investment-grade bonds and bond funds are probably the best for you

These are bonds issued by large, reputable companies, such as GlaxoSmithKline and Tesco. You are pretty likely to get your interest and your redemption payments from these players. This means that although the money is regular, it's not going to be as exciting as the junk bond possibilities.

## YOU LOVE THE IDEA OF HIGH REWARDS AND CAN COPE WITH HIGH RISK:

### Go for high-yield bonds

These are also known as junk bonds (they sound like rubbish but they're not necessarily). They could do really, really well but they're also more likely to tank at any moment. This is something on which you might like to risk a small portion (say 5%, or possibly less) of your portfolio.

Which of these is best for you depends upon what your portfolio needs to keep it diverse and how you feel about security/risk. So let's look at each type in turn.

# Very Safe with a Relatively Low but Dependable Regular Income

## GILTS

*Skill level: beginner to intermediate*

To reiterate: gilts are loans to the government. Just as you or I might go to a bank to raise a loan for a car or a mortgage for a house, the government comes to us, en masse, to raise some cash to spend on sensible things like trips to Brussels and nuclear warheads.

Personally I have not yet been able to bring myself to invest in government bonds of any sort. They seem so dull and offer such a low reward that I just can't be bothered. I think they are useful and sensible for people who have retired and want a fixed income (see page 164 for more on that) but for young investors, unless you're the sort who likes to wear two pairs of pants 'just in case', I think you could skip them.

It's a good idea to buy gilts direct rather than doing it through a fund. Not only do you avoid paying a management charge but gilts are exempt from capital gains tax if held directly. Short of the UK defaulting, you can be sure of your return at the outset.

### How they work

When you buy a gilt you are effectively lending money to the government and it promises to pay you a certain amount in interest each year for that loan. The interest is usually fairly low and can look very low relative to the interest rates you could get on savings bonds. However, at the time of writing (December 2009), gilts look rather good because the Bank of England base rate is so low that the interest we get on ordinary savings is pretty pathetic. Also, unlike savings bonds, which normally last for one to five years each, government bonds can last for decades.

Most gilts are issued for a fixed period of several years. What are called short-dated gilts are those with a period of up to five years before redemption (the date at which you are repaid), medium-dated are for those between five and fifteen years, and above fifteen years the gilt is known as long-dated. However you don't have to keep them for all that time. You can buy and sell them on the open market at any time.

There are also what are called 'undated gilts'. Undated gilts, as the name implies, are designed to carry on paying interest forever, without ever being redeemed. However, you have to be a bit careful with them, since they're not actually as undated as they sound and some could actually get redeemed in due course. They tend to have low interest rates and therefore their price tends to be quite a lot lower than £100.

Because gilts last such a long time, if you're thinking of buying into them you have to consider how you think the Bank of England interest rate will move in the future. This is because you could get a nice regular income simply by putting your money into savings accounts with banks or building societies.

If you think the base rate is likely to go up and stay up for a while then you could be better off putting your money into savings accounts. However, if you think interest rates could generally go down then a long-term gilt would be a good buy.

## The price of gilts

Gilts have a specific price at which you buy them, and that price is generally related to how impressive their interest rate seems at the time.

If basic Bank of England interest rates are low, the interest rates on bonds will look good so the price of gilts generally will be higher – in other words you pay a premium, more than 'par' (face value). This means that what you actually make overall on the bond (the amount it all adds up to when the term of the bond ends) will go down. However, if basic Bank of England interest rates go up then bond rates will look unimpressive so their price will fall (it will be sold 'under par') and therefore their overall bond yields will rise. For example, a bond with a face value of £100 might sell for £105, meaning at a £5 premium. Or, you might find a bond of £100 value selling at £95 meaning you bought at a discount.

When you come to redeem these gilts – in other words, when they come to the end of their terms – you will redeem them at £100. So if you bought them at £95 you will make money on the sale, if you bought them at £105 you will lose some. It's important, then, to make sure that bonds you buy 'above par' have enough of an interest rate payment each year to more than make up for the loss you make at the end.

## How to work out how much you will make

There are two main things you should consider if you buy gilts:

1. The price of the gilt (per £100 worth)
2. The coupon (interest rate) being offered

If a gilt is offering a low interest rate, relative to average rates for savings accounts, it's likely to be selling at a discount. So you could find that you only have to pay, say, £96 for £100-worth of a particular gilt. Or if the gilt's interest rate is looking rather attractive it might be selling at £106. Put it this way – if you're going to pay over 100p for your gilt you need to know that the interest you will get year-on-year will be good.

It's a choice for you – do you want to have the capital growth or do you want to have the higher interest payments?

You can invest as little as £1 in gilts but people generally buy them in multiples of £100 which is how they are displayed in the boring-looking columns in the financial pages of broadsheet newspapers. So, for example, if the government wanted to raise £1 billion to be repaid in 2020 with a fixed interest rate of 4.5% they would issue gilts called something like '4.5% Treasury 2020'.

### Don't forget inflation

Given that the interest rate of gilts is fixed – often for a long time (it could be decades) – do you think that it will cover inflation and beat average savings rates over that time? The longer your gilt lasts, the more of a gamble it is as no one can see into the future and no one can accurately predict the movements of interest rates over time.

You can get index-linked gilts where the interest paid and the redemption amount rise in line with inflation. In fact, it's not quite as good as this, because they lag inflation by three months. However, they can be a good option if you're planning on keeping your gilts for many years – the longer you keep a fixed-income investment the more it is affected by inflation.

Still, index-linked gilts, not surprisingly, tend to offer a lower interest rate than the fixed ones. Again, it's a gamble you have to consider and there are no definite answers. You will need to get your calculator out; work out the difference over time (assuming at least 2.5% inflation each year). If you're looking for low risk in your investments, it probably doesn't get much lower than this.

## How to buy gilts

You can buy gilts through most stockbrokers, just like you can buy shares. To purchase gilts directly, you need to apply and register with Computershare (https://www-uk.computershare .com/Investor/Gilts/Default .asp), an outsourced agent of the Debt Management Office (DMO).

You used to be able to buy gilts through the Post Office or direct from the Bank of England but you can't any more, which is a shame as buying through the Post Office seems a nice, easy way to do it to me.

Buying gilts, once you've done all of that, is reasonably straightforward. Occasionally, the government has new gilt issues, and they are often sold direct to the public either at a fixed price or by tender or auction. You can find out about forthcoming issues at the website of the government's Debt Management Office (Dmo.gov.uk). The advantage of buying a new issue of gilts is that there is no dealing commission, which cuts down on your costs.

I suggest you set up an online stockbroking account – an execution-only service – just as you would for buying shares (see page 317 for a list of online brokers). Instructing your broker to buy or sell gilts is similar to instructing them on shares:

- *You look for what the current market price is on a particular stock.*
- *You instruct your online broker to go ahead, either at a particular price or 'at best'.*
- *Your online broker service executes the trade on your account.*
- *You receive a contract note from your broker in the post. Apart from dealing commission, which may be a flat fee or a percentage of the deal value, the contract note may also show an adjustment for 'accrued interest' – the amount of interest that has accrued on the gilt since the last income payment.*

## GILT INDEX TRACKERS: NO THINKING REQUIRED, LOW COSTS AND A DEPENDABLE RETURN

*Skill level: beginner to intermediate*

Gilt index trackers provide a mix of gilts and stay in line with inflation. Gilts are conservative options at the best of times and buying into an index-linked gilt tracker won't exactly roll in the cash. But whether the economy is growing or shrinking, gilt index trackers are fairly solid, reliable investments.

Although initial fees are relatively low, minimum investments can be high (as much as £100,000). It is worth finding out which trackers are of interest to you, based on which index they are tracking and the companies that comprise the fund; contacting the issuer for more details if needed.

Once you're positive about your chosen tracker, the most cost-effective way to invest is through a fund supermarket (see below). Vanguard's UK government bond index, for instance, is offered through investment dealer Alliance Trust with an annual management charge of just 0.15% – unlike the 1% to 5% or more that managed bond funds would charge. The minimum investment is also substantially lower through this platform.

Here are some examples of gilt index trackers that are available:

- *Aviva BGI Over 15 Years Gilt Index Tracker*
- *Zurich BGI Index Linked Over 5-year Gilt Index Tracker ZP*
- *Scottish Widows Index-linked Gilt Tracker Fund*
- *iShares FTSE All Stocks Gilt Exchange Traded Fund*
- *Vanguard UK Government Bond Index*

## GILT TRADED FUNDS: USE A FUND SUPERMARKET OR AN ETF

*Skill level: beginner to intermediate*

An alternative to buying gilts or bonds directly is to invest in a unit trust that specialises in gilts. You can find a list of gilt funds on the website of the Investment Management Association (www.investmentuk.org).

The advantage of investing in a fund is mainly that your money will be spread across lots of gilts.

The disadvantage, as usual, is that costs can be high – as much as 6% on entry and 1.25% annually. These charges mean that the yield on your investment will be lower than the yield of the actual gilts in that fund, i.e. the fund managers are creaming off a chunk of the profit.

Some funds take their charges from the income and some take it from the capital. Be careful. The normal practice is to take it from income, but if a fund takes it from your capital, its yield will look artificially high. One way to cut down on these nasty management fees is to buy through a fund supermarket, also known as a fund wrap or fund platform.

## Fund supermarket
*Skill level: intermediate*

A fund supermarket provides a broad selection of all sorts of funds sitting next to each other, vying for your business by reducing fees and offering deals. There is also information relating to each fund that you can read as part of your selection process.

Be clear, though, that this is where you must be prepared to do that reading as well as other research. You don't have a fund manager making the selections for you, but then you don't end up paying the fund manager loads of money in fees for that help.

Fund supermarkets are good places to buy ALL types of funds. A very small selection of the plethora of fund supermarkets out there is:

- *Cofunds (Bestinvest)*
- *Vantage (Hargreaves Lansdown)*
- *Fundchoice*
- *FundsDirect (Fidelity)*

## Invest through an ETF

*Skill level: beginner to intermediate*

Even cheaper is to invest through an exchange-traded fund (ETF). As I mentioned in Chapter 4, exchange-traded funds are relatively new products and they are often the cheapest way to invest in shares, commodities, bonds and gilts.

What makes ETFs different from other types of fund (such as mutual funds) is the fact that they are traded on major stock exchanges, i.e. you can buy 'shares' in them in the same way that you can buy shares in a company. So if you decide to invest in them you would do so through a broker in the same way as you would if buying company shares.

Most ETFs will often track an index. They also differ from mutual funds in that they don't have an expensive fund manager at the helm. Therefore they're cheap and, generally, they work better than managed funds.

## HOW ARE ETFs PRICED?

ETFs are valued according to their NAV (net asset value) – the value of the fund's assets minus its liabilities – at the end of each trading day. They are described as open-ended, which means that shares can be bought and sold at any time and the price of single units of the fund will vary proportionately to its NAV.

A gilt ETF (an exchange-traded fund that invests in gilts) is a good option if you want to underpin a diverse portfolio with a solid holding that provides a steady income at regular intervals (something that I've recommended). It's not exciting, but it's pretty reliable.

There aren't a great deal of UK government bond exchange-traded funds out there, but you could investigate the following:

- *iShares FTSE All Stocks Gilt (LSE: IGLT)*
- *The shorter duration FTSE Gilts 0-5 (LSE: IGLS)*

Both charge just 0.2% a year. iShares also offer a Gilt ETF (INXG-LSE) that is linked to the UK government bonds index, and therefore would offset the risk of inflation.

# Safe with a Higher Return

## INVESTMENT-GRADE CORPORATE BONDS

Corporate bonds offer different levels of return depending on their credit rating (see 'Risk and Reward' on page 164). The corporate bonds I'm looking at here are 'investment grade', i.e. AAA, AA, A and BBB.

The higher the credit rating the lower the risk and therefore the lower the interest payments on the bond; the lower the credit rating the higher the risk of losing your money but the more interest you will earn.

There are two main ways of actually investing in corporate bonds. You can either select specific bonds yourself and buy them directly, or you can invest through some form of bond fund.

Most people do the latter because it's easier, generally safer (as with shares, it's safer to invest in a group of them and spread your bets than to place all your money on one single company) and you don't have to invest quite so much, on the whole.

## DIRECT PURCHASE OF CORPORATE BONDS

*Skill level: advanced*

If you are not a seasoned, sophisticated investor then buying bonds direct is probably not for you. It requires a great deal of knowledge and understanding, which tends to be hard to come by with bonds. It used to be that you also needed large chunks of money (e.g. £10,000–£50,000 per investment) to do it, but that has been made a little easier recently by the introduction of what is called the 'Retail Bond Platform' on the London Stock Exchange. You need a broker to buy them (although you can use the cheap, online, execution-only brokers listed on page 317) and the minimum investment is £1,000. Currently there are a limited number of companies you could invest with in this way, but keep an eye on it because it could grow substantially if it becomes popular.

Corporate bonds can be placed inside an ISA with all the advantages that that affords, but a beginner should really be using the ISA for other investments.

For the record, you can buy bonds through most stock-brokers. I recommend using a discount broker to invest in a fund or an online execution-only broker if you know exactly what you want to invest in. Price and credit ratings for some bonds are available at Bondscape.net.

A discount broker provides a stripped-down service and purely trades with your money at your request without the added benefit of investment advice. They charge a much lower commission than their full-service counterparts and are the popular choice with most investors.

Discount brokers have effectively made investing affordable and accessible. Don't be fooled by the 'discount' tag and assume that this is an inferior service. They support the DIY investor in his/her market endeavours, and in fact this should definitely be your first port of call (having done your research) when you look to invest.

Well-known firms such as

- *Hargreaves Lansdown (Hargreaveslansdown.com)*
- *Best Invest (Bestinvest.co.uk)*
- *Chartwell (Chartwell.co.uk)*

are good places to start.

## CORPORATE BOND FUNDS: SPREADING THE RISK BUT STICK TO INDEX TRACKERS AND ETFs

For all the same reasons that have been covered in the section on gilts, it is probably best for the less experienced investor to avoid a managed fund and, instead, buy bonds in an index tracker or ETF.

The key point to keep in mind with bond funds is the higher the rate of income they offer, the riskier their portfolio of investments will be (see 'Risk and Reward' on page 164). Risk is much more of an issue with corporate bonds than it is with gilts, which are pretty much rock solid.

## CORPORATE BOND INDEX TRACKERS: LITTLE THINKING REQUIRED, RISK IS REDUCED

*Skill level: beginner*

As you saw in the chapter on shares, index trackers are essentially funds that track the performance of a sector of the market, also known as an index. They are cheap to invest in as they don't have to pay Christmas bonuses to expensive City types, and their returns are reliable but not entirely safe from market turbulence.

With a bond index tracker you are less likely to have the 'boom and bust' element, so you are partly shielded from the market's volatility. The other side to that coin, though, is that you are less likely to get a fab windfall from a particular investment.

Corporate bond indices include:

- *Barclays Corporate Bond Index*
- *Citigroup US Broad Investment Grade Credit Index*
- *Dow Jones Corporate Bond Index*

## CORPORATE BOND ETFs: CHEAP BUT REQUIRES RESEARCH AND EFFORT ON YOUR PART

*Skill level: intermediate*

One of the best and cheapest ways to invest in corporate bonds is to do it through an ETF (Exchange-Traded Fund – see page 104 for more information on what these are and how they work).

ETFs are low-cost index-tracking funds, which can be traded daily and are exempt from stamp duty. There are 12 UK bond and gilt ETFs – for more information, see Londonstockexchange.com.

I really recommend this way to invest in corporate bonds – it is easy, cheap and no-fuss.

# High-Yield Returns

## JUNK BONDS: VERY RISKY WITH THE POTENTIAL OF A VERY LARGE RETURN

*Skill level: advanced*

Now we are looking at 'sub-investment grade' or junk bonds (also optimistically called high-yield bonds).

These are bonds that have been given a rating of BB or lower, i.e. they are risky. Remember, the lower the credit rating the higher the chances of the money not being paid back.

Junk bonds tend to be bought by investors who know a great deal about the company that is issuing the bond – its industry sector, its company numbers, its future. Either that or they're basically gamblers! The proper investor tends to buy a selection of different junk bonds from different companies and sectors in the knowledge that many (or even most) of the companies may default (i.e. not return the money or make the interim interest payments if there are any). But the investor knows that if, say, one in ten of the companies does well then the value of the bond shoots up so the investor can then sell the bond at a big profit.

Junk bonds are, in all likelihood, not for you as this book is aimed more at the relatively new or inexperienced investor. If you have a substantial and diverse investment portfolio and can afford to allocate a few thousand pounds on a bit of a gamble then junk bonds would be one of the options – but only after you've done some sustained and detailed research and become something of a specialist in which companies' bonds have, in your opinion, been given an unfairly poor rating.

# Types of Bonds to Avoid

These either require a level of skill and sophistication that isn't catered for in this book, or they are a waste of money.

### CONVERTIBLE BONDS: VERY COMPLEX

*Skill level: very advanced*

Convertible bonds are bonds that can be converted into shares at a later date. So they require an understanding of the share value of the company/industry sector, the point at which the bond can be converted, the opportunity cost of converting or not converting . . .

Best to stick to the basic bonds and gilts before you consider moving to more complex products like these, I think.

### PERMANENT INTEREST-BEARING SHARES (PIBS) AND PERPETUAL SUBORDINATED BONDS (PSBs): RESTRICTIVE AND UNATTRACTIVE

*Skill level: not worth bothering*

Some building societies have issued bonds known as perma-nent interest-bearing shares (PIBS). There are also bonds that were issued by building societies that then went on to float on the stock market. These are called perpetual subordinated bonds (PSBs).

Although these bonds can have enormous interest rates, I think they are basically dull and, frankly, a bit of a cheek. Why do building societies think they're so special they have different rules for their bonds, particularly that they don't have to have a fixed redemption date so that you're at the mercy of markets if you want to sell? How come they can renege on the deal while other companies can't?

Again, I would start with basic gilts and bonds before thinking about potentially investing in PIBS or PSBs.

# How Do I Actually Buy Gilts, Bonds, Funds or ETFs?

The way you choose to invest in types of bond-related investments will depend on how hands-on you can and want to be.

## EXECUTION-ONLY BROKERS: YOU'RE ON YOUR OWN (BUT IT'S CHEAP)

If you are willing to pick it up as you go along, execution-only online brokers are the way to go. You simply set up an online account with your desired firm (TD Waterhouse, Selftrade, E-Trade and Barclays are all big players; see page 317 for a list of them), in much the same way as you would set up an Amazon account.

You are then provided with an account ID, a PIN/password and a landing page on which you can manage your investments and execute trades yourself across international markets, dealing in sums as small or as big as your bank account will allow. You will usually be charged a flat fee per transaction, which can be as little as £9.95, and if you make more trades your monthly subscription might be reduced.

Brokers are at the end of the phone should you need them to buy stock or help you get started with your account, but his/her role doesn't extend much further than this; they are not on hand to provide you with investment advice.

Launching straight in and buying stocks aimlessly sounds daunting, and actually doing that would be a silly thing to do. But with prior research, your foray into the stock market can be fruitful.

The sites themselves usually contain loads of useful information for the first-time investor. Some will have jargon-busting pages and online tutorials, and some will even have a facility that allows you to trade with fictional money (paper trading) so you can get a feel for the highs and lows of the stock market. Look for an education or training facility on your chosen site before signing up.

Of course, the Internet is a great place to assess the performance of shares and markets, as well as seeing what other people are doing; message boards and forums are good places to pick up tips and talk to recent stock-market converts. Taking a keener interest in financial news and picking up on trends in certain markets will also help when you come to invest.

## FULL-SERVICE BROKER: HELP AT HAND BUT YOU PAY FOR IT

If you would feel more comfortable with a little guidance, you could enlist the services of a full-service advisory broker. These provide a comprehensive money-management service, advising on investment, dealing with your portfolio and even smoothing out tax issues.

'Great, sign me up!', I hear you say, but the reason I'm fleetingly suggesting advisory brokers is because they cost – oh yes they do! They charge portfolio management and maintenance fees as well as generous commissions, which go straight into the broker's pockets. These really do cost an arm and a leg, so you will need to weigh up whether you really want to pass the buck when it comes to researching your financial options. If you are totally clueless about the stock market and want total hand-holding it may be worth the investment. Prominent firms in this field include Prudential, Invesco and M&G.

## More Info About Bonds

While there are quite a few people around who understand shares, there are far fewer who understand how bonds work and there's not nearly so much information around either on the bookshelves or on the net about them. However, one useful website to read if you're interested in bonds and bond prices is Bondscape.net.

**What they want you to do:** buy packaged-up 'structured products' calling themselves 'growth bonds' or 'guaranteed bonds' or pretty much anything with the word 'bonds' in that sound safe and sensible but actually just make good money for the managers.

**What you should do:** invest in bond funds through ETFs or directly into gilts if you would like a very stable, moderate income.

Bonds may seem like a complex animal but they're certainly worth the effort of learning about them. Like stocks and shares, they don't need much managing on your part (unlike property, which we are going to look at in the next chapter) and if you buy them cheaply through an ETF you could be surprised at how well they do over the long term.

## Chapter 7

# Property

*Property Ladder! Homes Under the Hammer! A Place in the Sun?*
*Grand Designs?* British people have had a love affair with
property since the 1980s. It's not surprising really given that
from 1987 to 2007 property prices rose at an average rate of
7.7% per year.

The shine has come off property a little since the crash that
started in 2007. I knew a woman who bought a property every
six months, tidied it up, painted it white and put down cream
carpets – then sold each one on at whopping profit for most of
these years. Then came the crash. She got stuck and had to
sell off some of her properties at a loss. As lending criteria
tightened to a stranglehold through the credit crunch, house
prices tumbled and only regained slowly as lending improved
a little.

Long term, property in the UK is likely to continue to grow
in price and will probably outstrip inflation. No one can see into
the future but there are a number of factors that make it likely
that it will continue to increase:

- *We are a small island with limited space to build.*
- *Our population is growing due to an increased birth rate and immigration.*
- *We are living longer so more people are staying in their homes for longer.*
- *We are also increasingly living on our own and more single households put greater pressure on the housing stock than couples and families.*
- *The rate at which we are building new homes is not keeping up with demand.*

So, it is highly likely that property will increase in value, which is a very good reason for investing in it.

However, there are many good reasons why you shouldn't invest in it – at least not directly:

- *Property is effort. If you invest in shares or bonds, for example, other than keeping an eye on the market from time to time you don't have to do anything. With property, though, you have to do quite a lot of work, often hard, physical effort, unless you're willing to pay someone else, or a team of people, to maintain and run it for you. It can take a lot of your time and emotion, particularly if you are letting your property and get phoned at all hours by tenants with problems.*
- *If you own your own home that may be a high enough proportion of your money that is invested in the property asset class.*
- *There are many costs associated with property investment. Even if your property gains in value and/or brings in a decent rent each year you have to offset against that all the maintenance costs,*

*the upkeep, legal fees, tradespeople's bills, insurance and times when the property is empty for months and months. The big profits you see on the TV property shows aren't the end of the story.*

- *It is not liquid. You can't sell property overnight. Even the quickest transactions take weeks to complete. If you need money quickly you will have to drop the price substantially and even then, wait for the cash finally to come in.*

- *It is a volatile market. It might not seem as volatile as the stock market but it still has significant ups and downs. We have seen more of the ups in recent decades but it's easy to be caught in one of the downs and when it goes down it usually stays down for a long time.*

- *You have to put a lot of money in. Certainly you can borrow a lot to invest in property but you still have to put a large chunk of money down as a deposit, plus the other costs of buying a property. This may be too high a proportion of the money you have to invest to allow you to diversify your portfolio properly.*

- *Property is likely to go up at a much slower rate over the next 10 or 20 years than it has since the 1980s. No one knows, of course, but generally the opinion is that we're unlikely to see the rocketing prices that we have witnessed in the 1980s, the end of the 1990s and the mid-noughties.*

# Is Investing in Property Right for You?

The first question you have to ask yourself when considering investing money in anything is, 'Is this the best use of my time and money?' Have you better things to do than attend to blocked drains? Structural tests? Damp?

If you could make an equal or better return on your money by placing it in, say, a high-interest savings account or a tax-free ISA, then the only reason not to put your money in such an effortless and equal-paying alternative would be that you are passionate and knowledgeable about property, development, renovation and/or tenants.

So before you commit to buying property, find out what the best alternatives are that you could get from investing your money elsewhere. At the end of 2009, the best tax-free cash ISAs are hovering between 4.5% and 6%. So if you are looking to rent property out then your return (i.e. profit made after repairs, interest on debt, costs, allowance for empty periods) should be at least 10%. The 5% difference allows for the risk you are taking and time that you'll have to put in to finding and/or managing the property – time that you could otherwise use to make money elsewhere.

The other reason for making sure you have a much bigger return than on a passive investment is the changes in interest rates. If you are borrowing to part-fund your investment then you'd better be darned sure that a serious increase in interest rates of, say, 4% won't ruin you.

Yes, an interest rate hike of 4% or more in the lifetime of your project is possible – at the time of writing (December 2009) interest rates are at a low of 0.5%. There is only one way they can go. You have been warned!

'But,' you ask, 'what about the increase in value of the property while I'm renting it out?' Good question. But consider this: if you open an ISA and use it to invest in stocks and shares then you have a similar opportunity for 'capital growth', as it's called, but again with much less hassle on your part – stocks and shares don't need a new boiler, nor do they have raucous parties that damage your investment.

'But I want to have a property overseas that I can also use as a holiday home from time to time.' My honest answer to that is: 'Don't make your first property investment an overseas one no matter how siren the song of free holidays and cash in the bank. It doesn't work like that.'

To begin with you have to understand how to make a good investment in the property market. You also need to know how to manage and protect that investment. Add to all of that the difficulties of distance, language and cultural barriers, and it's more than a first-time investor should be taking on – unless they have family in that country or someone very successful and experienced guiding them.

By the way, that expert is going to charge for their knowledge, which could well wipe out any extra profit that you might have made. So you're probably back where you started!

## How to Calculate the Return on a Property Investment

The return on a property investment is, in very simple terms, what is left from the money you make from renting the property after you have covered the costs, interest payments and taxes that the project incurs.

The return is often referred to as the yield, i.e. how much your investment earns you year on year. This allows you to see whether it's worth subjecting yourself to the rigours of property investment for rental or if you might as well just stick to a much easier investment alternative.

This is where I shake my hair, shampoo-ad style, and say, 'Now for the maths bit!'

The yield on an ISA might be 5%. So if you were to invest £1,000 then you would earn 5% a year, i.e. £50 on that investment.

The yield on a property investment in its simplest form can be calculated as follows:

**Yield = (annual gross earnings – annual gross costs) ÷ initial total investment**

That is, total money earned annually on the investment – total costs incurred annually on the investment ÷ total-up front costs of obtaining the property.

So a property that cost £150,000 to buy and renovate (including interest, legal fees, etc.) might earn £20,000 a year in rental income but cost £5,000 a year to maintain (again including ongoing interest payments and all other costs). The formula for this example would look like this:

$$\text{Yield} = (£20,000 - £5,000) \div £150,000$$
$$= £15,000 \div £150,000$$
$$= 0.1 \text{ i.e. } 10\% \ (1 = 100\% \text{ so } 0.1 = 10\%)$$

The return varies depending upon the type of project you have in mind so I've given a rough guide of return for each of the following types of property investment at the beginning of each one.

There are three other crucial factors that you must get right as it's not just the money that you hope to make that you must take into account. If any of the following three factors is not lined up then you are in for a torrid time:

- *The amount you have to invest.*
- *How much risk you can afford to take.*
- *How much effort you are prepared to put in (think about that last episode you had with the dodgy plumber!)*

Learn to walk before you try to run. As I mentioned above, if you own your own home already (or at least if the bank does currently) then you may already have enough 'exposure' to property as an asset.

Not only that, but you could make money out of that asset without having to invest in anything else for the time being. For example:

- *Rent out your garage or driveway. If they're not in use all of the time – in particular free during office hours – then go to Parkatmyhouse.com or Parklet.co.uk and see what you could get for renting them out.*
- *Rent out storage space. Again, your garage could be rented out to others as storage space. So could your loft, your basement or your spare room. Advertise it on Gumtree.com or Spareground.com.*
- *Rent a room. The great thing about renting a room to another person is that the first £4,250 you earn per year is tax free. You don't have to have someone full-time or permanent either. You could rent to foreign students who only stay for about six weeks or you could rent to business people who only need to be with you on weekdays. The website Mondaytofriday.com is aimed at exactly those people.*
- *Rent the whole house. If you are particularly strapped for cash or you want to go away for many months then you could rent your entire home. The amount you would get entirely depends on the*

*property, the area and how long you are prepared to rent it for. Speak to local lettings agents to get an estimate on the possible rental income you could expect. You'll have to make sure any mortgage payments and maintenance costs are more than covered by the rental income otherwise it's probably a non-starter.*

For more information on how to go about making money from your home including the suggestions above and even on how to make money by renting out your home as a film set, read the relevant articles on Moneymagpie.com or my previous book *The Money Magpie* (Vermilion).

If I haven't put you off property investing completely, here are some of the main ways you could profit from property.

## Start Small: Garages, the First Step on Property Purchasing

There's little glamour here . . . but it's worth a think!

*Return: low to medium*

*Capital requirement: low*

*Risk: low*

*Effort: low to medium*

If you have (or can raise) a relatively small amount of money to invest, but not enough to buy a flat or house, consider investing in garages.

Now this may not conjure quite the vision you had in mind but this book is about making money first and then being as glamorous as you like when you spend it – not the other way around! A friend of mine owns lots and lots of garages. That's how he makes his money. They are low maintenance – no boilers, leaks or noise issues – and they are relatively cheap to buy.

Once you own a garage you can use it for one of three things:

- *To create free space elsewhere that you can use to make money.*
- *To rent for car storage.*
- *To rent out for general storage.*

## CREATING SPACE

If you've decided to rent out a room or your whole house then you may have so much stuff to store that a commercial storage facility is too expensive.

Alternatively you may find a garage that is out of town where the demand for a garage is low and the price relatively cheap. You can rent this garage and fill it with stuff both from your garage and spare room then rent both of those out – assuming you live in an area where the demand for renting your garage and/or room will bring in more money than renting the garage itself.

## RENT FOR CAR STORAGE

This is the obvious one and requires patience as the return comes in over a few years. It's basically buy-to-let, but with a garage rather than a home.

By buying a garage at say £25,000 or £10,000 and renting it out for £105/month or £42/month respectively, you will be earning a pre-tax yield of 5%. Assuming there were no changes in the market affecting your garage, recouping your investment would take 20 years. Thereafter it would be pure profit.

## Know your market

So much for the theory but how do you actually go out and select the right garage and method of money making?

The answer is that you absolutely must without exception know your market. If you don't you will lose money. This applies to all the investment ideas in this chapter.

By way of example I'm going to look at the buying-to-let aspect of garages. This requires the greatest amount of understanding and the principles can be applied to any other form of garage use.

## Six weeks of research

Yawn, I know . . . Yes, six weeks and that's a minimum. During this time you will need to study your target area in detail – it may be local, it may be somewhere that you feel offers an opportunity.

Local newspapers and property newspapers. Read these in detail EVERY every week. This will allow you to get a general idea of how much garages cost in different districts in your target area. It will help you zero in on the areas where there is sufficient demand to sustain what you are looking to do.

See for yourself. Go and see the garages that are available and how much is being asked for them – both to rent and to buy. Drive around the streets so that you are familiar with the area first hand. Become very well versed in where there is unsatisfied demand, what the condition of the garages tends to be and how that affects the prices.

Visit local lettings agents and find out where there is demand for parking facilities. They should know where there are residents who don't have, but would be prepared to pay for, parking facilities.

Search on the Internet to find out a) what garages are for sale or rent and what the asking prices are; b) what the competition is that you are facing from other people doing the same thing as well as commercial organisations offering a similar solution e.g. parking or car storage.

Sign up for relevant property newsletters and contact your local council and find out what garages they have that you might be able to buy or rent. There may be redundant space in fields or undeveloped land that you could consider for parking space.

After six weeks you will begin to understand:

- *Where people need garage facilities.*
- *How much they are prepared to pay for these facilities.*
- *How much the market rate for garages is in different areas.*
- *What the yield will be on an investment in one or more garages.*

It will also allow you to begin to understand what might look like a bargain on purely price terms but is, in fact, a disaster.

If your research shows that you can't make money in the target area then you can be pleased. You've just saved yourself endless frustration and hassle, not to mention a lot of money.

If it shows that you could potentially make money then you now understand what you are looking for so you can expand your geographic horizons and see if the profit margin can be found elsewhere.

Once you've discovered what the market rates for buying and renting garages are, go to your council and find out what future developments are planned – transport, housing, amenities and anything else that might bring about a change in demand for better or worse.

If you are ahead of the game and happen to know that a new railway station is being planned for an area then there may be commuters who will want to park near that station but not pay exorbitant station parking fees.

By buying a garage in that area you are ready for that increase in demand and with it, rental and sale rates of garages.

## Being a Developer: Renovate, Improve, Upgrade and Sell

*Return: low to high*

*Capital requirement: high*

*Risk: high*

*Effort: high*

This one is all about spotting a property, usually a domestic home, that can be extended, upgraded, renovated or improved in some way. Once that improvement has been made then you can put it back on the market to sell it (you hope) for lots more than the total you paid to buy it plus all the costs, charges, interest, etc.

We are now in the land of high risk but potentially high return. If you are entering the world of property at this level then you'd better be prepared to do a lot of research before spending any money in order to stand any chance of protecting your investment.

## THE TWO GOLDEN RULES

1) Know your market. It was essential to know your market when buying a garage for, say, £25,000. You are now responsible for an investment of £125,000 upwards so you'd better know your market very, very well indeed.

2) Be prepared to get your hands dirty. The margin you are hoping to make on this type of property investment depends upon improving the property you've bought. The more of this improvement work you can do yourself the less of your potential profit you are eating into.

## HOW TO DO IT

A friend of mine, Stewart, is a successful small-scale property developer. His is an excellent example so I shall follow it.

### Stage 1: Know your target market

Stage 1 is ONLY getting to know your market. It is not selecting a property. Your research of the market is ongoing until you no longer want to participate in this type of investment.

### Stage 2: View floor plans

Floor plans allow you to see how you can better use the space, what walls or entrances can be moved, how a studio flat can be turned into a one-bedroom flat by reducing the kitchen or bathroom areas, or by changing the heating system or removing cupboards.

If you are convinced you could add significant value to a property, by say 25% at least, then it's worth continuing.

### Stage 3: Visit the property

Is it a stinker? The sort of aspects you should be looking for include but are in no way limited to:

- *Proximity to amenities: town centre, railway station, schools*
- *Facilities: parking, garden, south facing*
- *Structure: is it sound? i.e. no subsidence, walls and floors are solid and stable*
- *Utilities: are the water, electrics and gas in good order?*
- *Danger: is there any asbestos e.g. insulation or tiling? Is there a large tree growing too close to the foundations? Is there a council plan to build a bingo hall or an offenders' institute nearby? Does the neighbourhood feel safe, clean and tidy?*

Remember: You make money when you buy the property not when you sell it. In other words you are looking to purchase a property that you will be able to sell on with minimum fuss and cost.

## Stage 4: Assess the costings

Here is a spreadsheet that Stewart used on a property that he did NOT purchase and redevelop.

| Cost estimate | |
|---|---|
| Purchase price | £335,000.00 |
| Minus mortgage of | 60.00% |
| | £201,000.00 |
| Requires deposit of | £134,000.00 |
| | |
| Stamp duty | £10,050.00 |
| Legal fees | £1,500.00 |
| Mortgage application & survey costs | £2,000.00 |
| | |
| Total purchase cost | £147,550.00 |
| | |
| Mortgage payments per month (interest only 6.9%) | £1,155.75 |
| Council tax | £400.00 |
| | |
| Mortgage payments for a six-month period | £6,934.50 |
| Council tax for a six-month period | £2,400.00 |
| | |

| | |
|---|---|
| Total purchase cost over six months (not including renovation costs) | £156,884.50 |
| | |
| Renovation costs | |
| Project manager | £20,000.00 |
| Labour | £20,000.00 |
| | |
| Clearance | £5,000.00 |
| Cleaning | £5,000.00 |
| Skips | £5,000.00 |
| Re-wiring | £10,000.00 |
| Re-plumbing | £10,000.00 |
| Under-floor heating | £4,000.00 |
| Roof | £1,500.00 |
| Windows | £15,000.00 |
| Floors | £20,000.00 |
| Front of property | £5,000.00 |
| Carpets and insulation | £5,000.00 |
| Plastering | £5,000.00 |
| Painting | £5,000.00 |
| Bathrooms | £5,000.00 |
| Kitchen | £15,000.00 |
| Structural work | £5,000.00 |
| Demolition | £5,000.00 |
| Basement conversion inc kitchen & shower | £12,000.00 |
| | |
| Total for renovation | £177,500.00 |
| | |
| Total costs for 6 months including renovation | £334,384.50 |

Importantly he set a schedule as part of the budget (clever boy). People new to this type of development often fail to realise that time is against them. As time ticks on it gets both more expensive (tradespeople and interest payments) and more demoralising – that zeal you felt for the project six months ago has long gone and now you are hating the whole process.

So why didn't he do it? He didn't want to over extend his borrowings and the recession was not going away. That is to say, even though he identified a very good opportunity to make half a million quid in profit, he decided against it because it didn't match the type of investment profile he was looking for, i.e. one with a lower level of risk.

This decision was made after he'd done all that work on researching the market, assessing the floor plans, visiting the property more than once and drawing up the costings spreadsheet. That hard work, self-discipline and cold, dispassionate business thinking is what you need if you are to enter into this type of property development and stand any chance of succeeding. Don't let emotion in and don't buy a property just because you think it's pretty. This is business and you must look at the numbers, not the rose trellis.

## Stage 5: Managing the redevelopment

You've assessed the costs and selected a property that won't fall down, offers you the opportunity to add value and will sell relatively quickly. You've gone ahead and bought it so now all you have to do is redevelop it.

Finding good tradespeople is a whole new skill set that you have to take on. The method recommended to me by one of the Moneymagpies whose father was a clerk of works was this:

- *Find one really good skilled tradesman (e.g. roofer, electrician, plumber – not a 'builder') through recommendation and do not go with someone who is the cheapest.*
- *Get that person booked well in advance to come and do a specific job.*
- *Assuming they do show up and do a decent job, get every contact you can out of them for all the other jobs you need doing. With luck the people they recommend will also be reliable and good.*
- *Now go back to the first step and repeat as you'll need several people as backup for when others are unavailable/suddenly no longer there.*

This will not prevent the inevitable vanishing tradesperson act, but it will make you better prepared to cope with it.

The other major aspect to managing a project is to have time targets. These need to be realistic so that the tradespeople are not fleecing you, and similarly so that you don't have ridiculous expectations of what they can achieve. Also get the tradespeople to put in writing exactly what you have agreed they are going to do so that there are no disagreements down the line.

*MEMO*

This is an efficient idea that's rarely thought of but worth its weight in diamonds: if you don't have a sufficient budget to get a professional project manager in then pay one to act as a consultant whom you can phone from time to time for advice. At the very least pay one to give you advice on how to manage the project before you start. This will prove to be a very wise investment that will, in all likelihood, save you a bunch of money in the long run.

### Stage 6: Doing as much grunt work as you can

Knocking down walls (non-supporting ones only – watch *Fawlty Towers*: 'The Builders' if you want to see what not to do), removing rubble, clearing gardens or decorating do not require a great deal of skill so why pay a skilled tradesperson to do them?

Grunt work is not much fun but if you want to protect your margin of return then making space for rubbish or learning how to do tiling are 'musts'. What's more, any task you do yourself is something that can happen when you want it to, e.g. over a weekend, so that the next stage of development isn't held up. Time is money.

### Stage 7: Preparing the house for resale

Here is a big lesson that so many of those people on TV shows seem to miss: the property is not for you to live in, so don't style it to your taste. Style it to appeal to the target market. This is an area where an estate agent can actually be useful (unlikely but true). They will know what has broad appeal so check with them before you do the decorating or start spending £1,000 on a tap when a £150 tap would do just as well.

# Become a Landlord: Buy-To-Let

*Return: medium*

*Capital requirement: high*

*Risk: medium to high*

*Effort: high*

This property money-maker has a great deal in common with renting a garage and developing a property to sell on. You have the opportunity to make money down the line if you select the right property to begin with.

So as part of your research process, as outlined in the property development section, you also need to spend a good amount of time talking to letting agents and visiting rental properties. This will allow you to develop a very clear idea of what people want, where they want it, and how much they are prepared to pay for it.

Ask yourself who you want to rent to. Students require a lower standard of living but are far less respectful of your property. Professionals are pretty much the reverse of that formula.

As a basic rule you can reckon on needing to spend less up front on a student property to let and making a higher yield. But you can expect more hassle from student tenants – property damage, upsetting neighbours, vacant property during summer.

Your starting point is how much you have to invest. This will enlighten your research so that you can find out what rental market you can target in your chosen area. If necessary you can then look elsewhere and see if you have more options in a locality where the property is generally cheaper.

Select a property to which you can add value, though. That way should you be under any financial pressure you can sell part or all of the property and generate a lump of money to reduce debts or sort out whatever the challenge was.

The other reason for selecting a property to which you can add value is that it means your initial total investment is lower and, therefore, your yield will be higher – see the examples below.

> Example 1: property in great condition and ready to rent out
> Total purchase investment: £175,000
> Annual rental receipts (after annual costs): £15,000
> Yield: 8.6%
>
> Example 2: identical property requiring improvement
> Total purchase investment: £150,000
> Improvement costs (including work done by you to keep costs down):
>   £10,000
> Total up-front investment: £160,000
> Annual rental receipts (after annual costs): £15,000
> Yield: 9.4%

The higher the yield the sooner you make all your money back and are into pure profit.

As part of the research and selection process (outlined above), you will need to put a spreadsheet together. Only this time you are not looking at just a quick turnaround and lump-sum return. Now you are looking at a longer-term investment with an ongoing income stream.

The following is an actual spreadsheet for a property that was purchased, redeveloped and let out.

| RENTAL PROPERTY COSTS | |
|---|---|
| Purchase price | £335,000.00 |
| Deposit % | 30% |
| Deposit amount £ | £100,500.00 |
| Stamp duty | £10,050.00 |
| Mortgage amount £ | £234,500.00 |
| Mortgage rate % | 7% |
| Mortgage payment (per month) | £1,367.92 |
| Mortgage payment (per year) | £16,415.00 |
| Build cost per flat | £20,000.00 |
| Number of flats | 7 |
| Total build cost | £140,000.00 |
| Total cost (inc 1 year's mortgage) | £266,965.00 |
| Value after conversion (per flat) | £131,428.57 |
| Value after conversion (whole property – 7 flats) | £920,000.00 |
| Rental income (per month) | £4,200.00 |
| Rental income (per year) | £50,400.00 |
| GROSS PROFIT IF SOLD | £653,035.00 |
| ANNUAL GROSS PROFIT IF RENTED | £33,985.00 |

## THE REALITY OF THE TENANT

Every time a tenant moves in there is the hassle of the inventory and various bits of paperwork to sort out. Deposits now have to be placed with a separate independent organisation. Bins and bicycles mysteriously appear where they shouldn't and noise does have a tendency to carry. Leaks happen, there are drainage problems, burst boilers, washing machines that don't work and angry ex-boyfriends who kick the door in.

So the lesson to learn here is not to buy the cheapest shower pan, bed, furniture, etc. Whatever you equip the property with has to be able to withstand the rigours of a tenant who doesn't really care because it's not their property.

What's more the property, if being converted for rental or even just refurbished and continued for rental, has to have a sound insulation test. This costs a stupid amount of money and can only take place after you have finished the whole building, i.e. when it is too late to cheaply fix or improve the sound insulation measures you have taken.

## HEALTH AND SAFETY

And there's more. The furnishings have to be fire retardant. The doors have to be fire doors. If there was a fire alarm system in the building it has to be maintained, i.e. expensive visits on a frequent and regular basis by a registered inspector.

Similarly gas (often avoided completely by many landlords for this very reason) has been known to give rise to carbon monoxide leaks or even explosions.

These and many, many more exciting issues are covered by both your local council and National Landlords Association (Landlords.org.uk), Residential Landlords Association (Rla.org.uk) and National Federation of Residential Landlords (Nfrl.org.uk).

This brings us right back to doing your homework and making sure that you are selecting a property that allows you to add value. That way if you want out of the rental game you can leave with some profit.

# Buying Overseas, Listed Buildings and Other Nightmares

*Return: medium*

*Capital requirement: high*

*Risk: high*

*Effort: high*

I'm only going to touch briefly on these because, frankly, you shouldn't touch them unless you are already experienced with property purchase and development.

## OVERSEAS PROPERTY

Wouldn't it be nice to own a place by the sea, on the Mediterranean? No hassle of finding somewhere to stay each year or fighting the crowds. Ah joy.

It's a lovely dream but that's all it is – a dream. The reality is that you have all the trials and tribulations of any property purchase or development but with much greater challenges and much higher risk. There are enough TV shows that have covered the horrors of the disappointment and misery of a poorly (or sometimes well) planned foreign venture to give you an idea of what it can be like.

As well as the research process outlined above, you now have to add in the distance, language and cultural challenges. Not only that, but there are often higher costs for foreigners buying properties in various different countries. Depending on where you buy you could find yourself effectively penalised for being foreign.

How often are you going to be able to get over there to drive the project along? Do you speak the local language fluently enough to be able to convey technical building terms? Do you fully understand the pace of work in that locality and how thoroughly different it is likely to be from what you'd expect in your home town?

Instead, take the money you are looking to 'invest' in an overseas property and put it into an investment that you can control and understand. Then use the profits to pay for your overseas holidays. Much better.

## LISTED BUILDINGS, CONSERVATION AREAS, UNUSUAL PROPERTIES

Again avoid them until you really know what you are doing in the property market. You already have to deal with building regulations, planning permission and picking the right property so as not to lose all your money. Don't make it even harder by buying something in which you can't cough without written approval in triplicate.

# Indirect Property Investments

*Return: low to high*

*Capital requirement: low to high*

*Risk: low to high*

*Effort: low to medium*

Why so vague? I hear you ask. Well, as the 'low to high' ratings above indicate, there are many variations within the term 'indirect investments'. It's all about deciding what you are looking for in terms of the amount you are prepared to invest, the level of risk you are prepared to accept, and how much yield you expect in return.

An 'indirect property investment' is mainly about investing in property funds. Rather than purchasing a property yourself, you place your money with property investment 'experts' who invest the money on behalf of a group of investors.

There are three main types of indirect property investment and, to be brutally honest, I'm not a big fan of any of them:

- *Syndicates*
- *Shares of property companies or funds*
- *REITs*

The advantages of investing your money in this way (such as they are) are mostly to reduce your level of risk and certainly the amount of effort you have to put in. Assuming that you do your research and speak with a good IFA (an independent one, of course), by placing your money with a syndicate or a specialist property fund you:

- *Have the expertise of the investment managers working for you.*
- *Have the opportunity to spread your investment across a number of different property types and locations.*
- *Can avoid putting your entire investment into one property which, if it doesn't make money, could ruin your financial position.*

So let's have a closer look at them.

## SYNDICATES

To all intents and purposes joining a property syndicate is much the same as investing money in a portfolio of shares for the following reasons:

- *You have to be very clear about what sort of investment you want to make.*
- *You have to be prepared to do a heck of a lot of research to make sure that you find a trustworthy syndicate that offers good returns.*

---

### RISK AND RETURN

Before you look into this one any further be aware of this: property syndicates are not covered by the Financial Services Authority. This means that they are not bound by rules of behaviour laid down by the authority. So these funds are, by default, higher risk than your average investment fund opportunity, which is covered by certain rules and procedures. That said, any property you invest in is also not covered by the FSA so just by stepping into the world of property investment in any of the ways I have covered in this chapter so far you are moving up the risk ladder.

---

### Types of syndicate

The two main types of syndicate are:

- *Structured return*
- *Profit share*

The former is less risky and therefore offers a lower return, some or all of which has been agreed in advance. The latter depends entirely upon the success of the venture but can, if you select very carefully and are happy to take on risk, pay substantially more.

There is no end to the variation on what the syndicate chooses to invest in (UK or abroad, domestic or commercial). Also the timescales vary from around 18 months to 10 years or more – so make sure you pick one that matches the period within which you are happy not to have access to your money.

### Pros and cons

The good news is that you don't have to worry about the management or ownership of the properties in which the investment is being made.

The bad news is that you don't have control over the management or ownership of the properties in which the investment is being made.

## A GOOD SYNDICATE WILL:

- *Allow you to invest a smaller amount of capital than you would have by investing in a property on your own, i.e. you are only coughing up £25,000 as opposed to £125,000.*
- *Give you a higher potential return because of the greater buying power of between four and twenty people all pooling their resources and being able to get discounts on purchases.*
- *Give you a higher potential return because of leverage. For example, if you bought a property for £50,000 the yield would*

*probably be fairly low, say 5%, i.e. 5% of £50,000 is £2,500. However, by being part of a syndicate you could invest the same £50,000 which would be part of a bigger investment and more likely to command a higher yield – perhaps 10%, and 10% of £50,000 is £5,000.*

- *Provide expertise and experience in selecting the property project(s) in which to invest.*

## A BAD SYNDICATE WILL:

- *Run off with your money never to be seen or heard of again.*
- *Give you a poor return because they invested badly and charged you every time they moved.*

In other words, all that research you would have done on selecting a property in which to invest on your own, you now apply to selecting the right property syndicate to invest in.

### Knowing what you want

Before you start looking for a property syndicate to join you need to decide how much risk you are prepared to run on this investment and how much return that will earn you (if all goes well).

Next you have to decide how much money you are prepared to invest in a syndicate. There is no strict minimum or maximum amount to invest but £25,000 seems to be the minimum buy-in for many syndicates.

As always a basic necessity is to go online and do lots and lots of searching. Check the newspapers, Fool.co.uk, Investorschronicle.com, Thisismoney.co.uk and develop a clear understanding of what syndicates expect from you and what they offer in return.

## Sifting through the syndicates

Having done that, now would be a good time to find an Independent Financial Adviser who specialises in property investments. It may take some time to find one but they are out there. Try Unbiased.co.uk for a list of those that do cover this area but don't just go for the first one you find. Check out at least three of the IFAs you find on there before choosing one. (NB When looking on Unbiased untick the box that says 'Display only IFAs that have website and email links' – those IFAs are paying for those links and you want IFAs that don't need to pay to get clients.)

Ask to buy an hour or two of their time and send them a brief of what you want out of them, ideally with the results presented in person.

The brief will include the following:

* *The investment you are looking to make*
* *The level of risk you are prepared to take (i.e. very safe, safe, risk, high risk, etc.)*
* *The level of return you want*
* *The information you want from the IFA, namely a list of longstanding, reliable syndicates that offer what you want*

As a fail-safe you may also want to make it clear that you will not be investing straightaway (so there's no point in trying to get you to spend money through them cos it ain't going to happen); and that you want the majority of syndicates on the list to be ones with which the IFA doing the search has no commission or payment relationship, i.e. the IFA will not be biased by potential commissions that he or she could earn by sending you to specific syndicates on your list.

Next telephone all of the syndicates and ask them for their prospectus for future investment projects and performance of all their syndicated property investments over the past 10 years.

As well as giving you the information you are asking for this will also tell you what they are like to deal with – do they answer the phone quickly? Are they polite? Do they send the information you ask for? Do they send it quickly?

Remember you are considering investing at least £25,000 or so with these guys so they'd better behave themselves if they want your money!

### Shortlist

You should be able to pare the longer list down to a shortlist of three to five syndicate projects. The thing to do then is really know in detail what each syndicate offers. Then telephone each of the syndicates on the shortlist and speak to one of their account managers (or someone who can answer your questions).

Tell that person what advantages you have in other syndicates and ask them to explain why theirs is the better option. This will tell you all sorts about their integrity and ability to cope with you as a client as well as what is good or bad about their syndicated project(s).

Then you have to decide which one best serves your needs. As a further fail-safe you can get the original IFA (or another one if you want a second opinion) to advise you where you should invest your money among the shortlist you have made. As you can see, there's a lot of effort involved in this and even at the end there is no guarantee that you will make good money. Sometimes it's better simply to go off and buy a flat to rent out.

## SHARES IN PUBLICLY TRADED PROPERTY COMPANIES

There are plenty of publicly listed companies whose primary interest is to make money through property. They tend to focus on long-term modest returns earned from commercial tenants. For example they might own a shopping centre, in which case they will have their tenants (the retail stores) sign leases typically of at least three years – very often ten years or more.

So the emphasis is on finding and maintaining good tenants who are likely to pay rent reliably year on year, not on looking for a property that can be resold quickly at a substantial profit. Some of these companies, in terms of the property they own, are colossal – British Land and Land Securities are two of Britain's biggest, owning between them around £8 billion worth of property assets.

The trouble with property companies as an investment option is firstly that the share prices tend not to reflect the value of the company and secondly (partly the cause of the first problem) if you own shares in these companies you are subject to double taxation. That is, the company is taxed on corporation and capital gains tax and then any dividends or share value increases you earn will be subject to your personal income tax and capital gains tax.

This applies whether or not you invest in an investment company or an investment fund, i.e. a company whose only activity is buying and selling shares in property companies.

So what do you do? Well, if you want to invest in shares (and you really should give it some serious thought) then read Chapter 4 again. However, there is a cunning alternative by the name of Real Estate Investment Trusts.

## REAL ESTATE INVESTMENT TRUSTS (REITs)

Back in the 1880s the good old US of A decided that double taxation on property shares was unpopular. REITs (pronounced 'reets') were developed as the solution. Quick as ever, the British government saw the advantages of this concept and developed its own REIT legislation a mere 120 years later.

As it happens, the introduction of REITs in the UK could not have been worse timed, coming as it did at the beginning of the biggest recession and related property slump in decades.

Anyway, ignoring the fact that REITs are currently paying a worse dividend than a good cash ISA (as of December 2009, 16 out of 20 are paying less than 6% – see www.reita.org/live/Databank/databank_reits.html for up-to-date info), there are a few reasons to keep REITs in mind as a possible investment target (though not many).

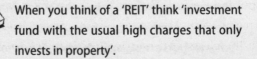

When you think of a 'REIT' think 'investment fund with the usual high charges that only invests in property'.

## The features and benefits of a REIT

- *REITs are tax free (at the company level). This is the big one. A REIT is not subject to corporation or capital gains tax. So if the REIT makes a profit by selling and/or managing property then it can distribute that profit without any of it being taken by Inland Revenue. So there should be more money to spread among the shareholders – who do pay personal taxes as normal. However you will still be charged the 0.5% stamp duty for share purchases though this is less than you might be charged for a property purchase depending upon its value.*

- *Tax-free wrappers can be used. In other words you can use your ISA, SIPP, PEP or child trust fund to invest in a REIT and thereby have a 100% tax-free investment. (Bear in mind what I'll talk about in Chapter 8 regarding not letting the tax tail wag the investment dog.)*

  *In addition, 90% or more of the profits must be passed on to the shareholders. This is designed to make sure that the tax-free status of the REIT is used to the benefit of the shareholders (us common folk) and not the pin-striped City people who own and run the REIT. Shame it hasn't yet worked.*

- *High liquidity (i.e. it's easy to turn what you have into cash). By making these shares more attractive through lower tax, you can sell them quickly. Certainly a great deal more so than a position in a syndicate, a house or other piece of property in which you might alternatively place your money. In fact, one of the big selling points of REITs has always been that it is a more liquid property investment than investing in actual bricks and mortar.*

- *Access to commercial property. Almost everything else in this chapter looks at residential property. The reason for this is that if you want to invest in the commercial sector you either need to*

*join a syndicate (see above) or be in possession of several million*
*pounds. A REIT allows you to place some investment in the*
*generally speaking steady return world of commercial property.*

## What's REIT about it – and what's wrong

A REIT can be less hassle than buying, developing and reselling
or letting a property. You can place a smaller investment in a
REIT and thereby lower your exposure to the property market
– or indeed to a single property, if that's your alternative.

In theory it's tax efficient at least as far as the profits are
concerned. That's not to say that the people running the REIT
aren't taking a hefty fee for salaries, property management fees,
target incentives, champagne lunches and so on. Those are all
costs that are covered before any profits are dished out.

Those costs don't occur if it's your own property.

REITs are supposed to enhance the property sector of the
economy and thereby stimulate growth for all. However, two of
the very largest REITs are backed by the property giants,
British Land and Land Securities. Thankfully for them and their
investors the share prices in their REITs have recovered
substantially (34% and 35% respectively) in mid-2009.

But, at the time of writing (December 2009), over the last 10
years their share performance equates to:

British Land – up 2%
Land Securities – down 22%
(Source: 'A tale of two property giants', Owain Bennallack,
14 August 2009, Fool.co.uk)

And it gets worse. For nine of the last ten years inflation has hovered between 2.5% and 3%, falling dramatically in the last 12 months. If prices are rising at 2.5% and your investment is paying 2% then you are throwing 0.5% away every year – tax free or not.

So does that make now an excellent time to snap up bargain REITs shares or is it a mug's game because the 'experts' clearly have no more idea than you or me?

Frankly, I have never liked the idea of REITs, primarily because they are managed funds commanding offensive fees that cut into potential profits. They're generally fairly opaque and, as the past 10 years have shown, they really haven't done well. If you're desperate to get into property and can't afford a deposit on a buy-to-let then you might want to take a punt, but otherwise, I'd move on to something cheaper and better-performing if I were you.

> **What they want you to do:** invest in REITs or any other packaged-up, high-charging, opaque property fund.
>
> **What you should do:** think about whether you want to invest in property at all. If you do, do it in a straight-forward way that you can afford and manage either in garages, buy-to-let or simply letting a room or parking space to make extra cash.

## USEFUL RESOURCES

Websites
- Property: www.findaproperty.com, www.fish4homes.co.uk, www.houseprices.co.uk
- Local newspapers: www.newspapersoc.org.uk, www.daltonsproperty.com, www.loot.com
- Property for returns: www.designsonproperty.co.uk
- Landlords associations: www.landlords.org.uk, www.rla.org.uk, www.nfrl.org.uk
- Letting agents: www.naca.co.uk, www.arla.co.uk

Books
*Which? Essential Guide to Renting and Letting*
*Which? Essential Guide to Buying Property Abroad*

So, as you can see, although there are advantages to investing in property, other than the one you live in, there are many disadvantages including, most particularly, the time, effort and ongoing costs you have to bear. Owning property is often a job of work. Be prepared for the effort.

## Chapter 8

# Taxation – The Simple Way to Pay What You Have to and No More

You lucky thing . . . I've devoted a whole chapter to taxation not because it's so important but because it's . . . well, important. It's not something you should worry about every week (although you will find that the more you make the more it will start to bug you), but it has enough of an effect on your investments and your wealth over time to be worth considering sensibly at least a couple of times a year. Make sure you at least skim this chapter at some point. Tax is a fact of life and the more you understand about it the less you should have to pay.

There are a few basics that you need to know (and just keep an eye on as it changes) about the joyous – nay euphoric – subject of taxation. This chapter will cover the 'need to know' stuff. Of course, if you do become fascinated by the subject (and gosh, who wouldn't be – it's almost as exciting as insurance) and would like more practical advice about all aspects of taxation then dip into Jane Vass's book, *Daily Mail*

*Tax Guide*, or scour the tax office's websites starting with hmrc.gov.uk, which are surprisingly clear and helpful if you get to the right bits.

This chapter will cover the main areas where taxation will affect your savings and investments. You don't need to know it all off by heart, just have an idea in the back of your mind what kind of tax you may need to pay on some of them and how you could minimise your tax spend this year and in the future.

It's worth keeping up-to-date each year with changes that the Chancellor announces in the Budget (you don't have to watch the whole tedious parliamentary session, just get the main bits from the newspapers or websites the day after) because there could be at least one announcement that will necessitate a change in your investment plans.

## TAX AVOIDANCE VS TAX EVASION

Tax avoidance is perfectly legal. You are moving your money to where it gives you the best return while keeping the tax due to a minimum. But where tax is due you pay it on time.

Tax evasion is illegal. It is simply not paying taxes that you owe. Being paid in cash and not declaring that payment is an example. In fact receiving any interest payments, returns or other income and not declaring it is evasion. Don't do it!

# Two Main Points to Keep in Mind

1. Always use tax-efficient investments where they make sense

but ...

2. Don't let the tax tail wag the investment dog. In other words, don't invest in something simply because it has little or no tax attached to it. If the basic investment isn't going to bring you much in the way of rewards, then it's not worth it. Better to invest in something that gives you big returns with the commensurate offensive levels of tax if the net result (i.e. income minus tax) is more profit for you.

For example, you could put £1,000 in a tax-free savings account with the Post Office at, say, 5% interest earning you £50 a year. Or you could invest that £1,000 in shares that you think will grow by 15%. If you are right then you'll earn £150 that year minus 40% tax leaving you £90.

# Other Important Points to Remember

## CHECK YOUR TAX CODE

Make sure that you are on the right tax code for your general, non-savings tax. Your tax code is three numbers followed by a letter and is calculated by adding up all your allowances and then taking away the deductions from this total, such as tax on perks like company cars.

At the time of writing, most people in the UK who are below the age of 65 and in full-time paid employment have the tax code 647L. If you add a zero to the end of the three numbers, you get the amount you're allowed to earn in a tax year before you pay tax, so for the the allowance before income is taxable is £6,470. This is subject to change depending on what the Chancellor sets as the basic personal tax threshold in the Budget.

If your tax code is higher, it could be because you're in receipt of various forms of tax credits or other allowances, such as an age-related tax level. If your tax code is lower, it could be the taxman believes you're getting a perk via your employer, such as private health insurance, and so your personal allowance is lowered to offset the cash benefit you're deemed to receive.

Tax codes change when the Chancellor of the Exchequer changes the lower limit you have to earn before paying tax so it's worth checking each year.

If you think your tax code is wrong, contact your local tax office. Once you talk to someone at the tax office and tell them you believe you've been allocated the wrong tax code, they should be able to tell you how to proceed.

## KEEP ALL RECEIPTS, STATEMENTS AND BITS OF PAPER FOR SIX YEARS

As a general rule it's important to keep records (ideally paper records) of all types of income including gains from the sale of assets each tax year. Keep them for at least six years (this in fact is a legal requirement, and you could be fined if you fail to produce legible proof on demand). Invest in some sort of filing system so that you can look things up easily, particularly in case of a tax inspection . . . It doesn't always happen to other people!

## FIND A GOOD ACCOUNTANT

If your personal and tax affairs become complicated it will be worth employing a good accountant to help sort it out. That's not as straightforward as it sounds. Accountants, in my experience, vary from the brilliant to the criminally incompetent.

So the ideal is to get one that is qualified and recommended to you by someone who knows what they're talking about from personal experience (that bit's also important I've found). Make sure you have someone with professional accountancy qualifications or those from the Chartered Institute of Taxation (Tax.org.uk) or the Association of Tax Technicians.

## SELF-ASSESSMENT FORMS (THE MOST FUN YOU CAN HAVE WITH A TAXATION FORM)

Most people will be able to fill in their self-assessment form themselves each year (you can get help by logging on to www.hmrc.gov.uk/sa). And here are some important deadlines to keep in mind:

- *31 October: this is the deadline for those who receive a notice to complete their tax return by 31 July. If you fail to meet this cut-off date you'll be charged an automatic £100 penalty.*
- *30 December: this is the deadline by which you have to pay your tax if you owe less than £2,000 AND you want your tax to be collected through your tax code.*
- *31 January: this is the deadline by which you have to pay your tax if you don't want your taxes collected through your tax code and want to file your returns online. If your tax payment arrives with the Inland Revenue after this deadline you'll be charged an*

*automatic £100 penalty. If you are a further six months late you'll be charged another £100.*

# Paying Off Your Mortgage

As I mentioned in Chapter 2, one of the big advantages of over-paying your mortgage is that the money is invested tax free. So, if you had £5,000 to put somewhere, you could put it in a savings account at 5% but you would have to pay 20% tax on it giving you a real return of 4%. If you are a 40% taxpayer your real return would be 3%. However, if your mortgage were costing you 5% and you put that £5,000 into paying some of that off, you would benefit from the full 5% saving. The tax office sees paying off your mortgage as what it is, the payment of a debt, and therefore it doesn't tax you on your gain.

As I also mentioned in that chapter, as far as I am concerned, paying off your mortgage is one of the safest investments around. It gives you wonderful freedom and extra money each month to invest in long term once it is paid off. However, many investors disagree. They say that as your mortgage is pretty much the cheapest form of borrowing you will find, once you have stopped being a student, you are better off keeping that going and putting extra money, instead, into investments that should bring in an average of 10% a year over time.

On paper they are quite right, particularly if you factor in the power of compounding interest, but all of those investments, including even savings accounts, are less secure than paying off your mortgage. Also, all but the ones wrapped in ISAs attract tax which, in some cases, could bring down their real value to the price of your mortgage anyway.

Ultimately it's up to you. You might like to do a mix and pay off some of your mortgage but continue to put money in other investments at the same time, just slightly less each year. Or, if you are quite goal-oriented like me, you might actually enjoy the challenge of seeing how quickly you can pay off this big mother of a debt!

## FOREIGN INVESTMENTS

I have assumed through this book that you are resident and, for tax purposes, 'domiciled' in this country. There is a difference for tax:

Being 'resident' means that you are physically present in the country for at least 183 days or more in the tax year, while being 'domiciled' means you are in the country where you have your permanent home. Domicile is distinct from nationality or residence. You can only have one domicile at any given time. However, you could also be 'resident in the UK for tax purposes' but 'domiciled abroad'. 'Ordinarily resident' means that you live in the UK year after year – for at least 183 days or more.

If you're not any of these things, your tax situation will be different and I suggest you refer to Jane Vass's useful *Daily Mail Tax Guide* which is updated each year and explains what your tax liabilities are in this country. Also go to Hrmc.gov.uk or Direct.gov.uk or contact the tax authorities in your own country. If you are resident and domiciled in the UK and you have foreign income it is taxable here I'm afraid. You can claim relief for any foreign tax you have already paid, though. That includes income from an offshore bank or savings account, dividends on investments in foreign shares or a foreign pension (you are only taxed on 90% of a foreign pension).

# Taxes You Need to Care About

The four main taxes you need to consider when it comes to investing are:

- *Income tax (including savings tax)*
- *Capital gains tax (CGT)*
- *Stamp duty*
- *Inheritance tax (IHT)*

It's unlikely that you will be able to avoid paying all of these taxes. Even if you only have a bit of cash in a savings account you will still be taxed on the interest on that, unless you're a non-taxpayer and have filled in form R85 (info on that further down).

However, there are many and various ways of reducing your tax bill and, in some cases, avoiding paying tax at all on a few of your investments.

# Income Tax (Including Savings Tax)

After our own personal income allowance (£6,475 in the tax year 2009–10), anyone under 65 has to pay tax on earnings above that level. Even the interest on savings accounts is taxed at 20% before you see it, unless you are a non-taxpayer and have filled in the form R85 (available at all banks and building societies or online at: www.hmrc.gov.uk/forms/R85.pdf).

There is also a 10% tax on the dividends of shares and, again, this has to be paid by everyone, even if you have your shares in an ISA. However, the capital gain on your shares (the amount it grows in total value) is not taxed if it is kept in an ISA, as you will discover later in this chapter.

For higher-rate taxpayers, those that pay 40% on their income, it can be worth going for investments that don't incur tax on earnings such as National Savings & Investments products. However, you need to look at the total net return to work out if it's worth it. For example, if you have an investment that will give you 5% and you have to pay 40% tax on it you will really make 3%. But if you have a non-taxable investment that gives 2.5% you would still be better off investing in the taxable product.

If you're married or in a civil partnership, it's helpful to put many investments in the name of the lower earner as they are likely to pay less, or even no, tax on them.

## RENTAL INCOME

Tax on income from property – including buy-to-let properties and holiday lets (based in the European Economic Area) – is paid on the net profit you make after you subtract allowable expenses.

Allowable expenses include:

### For holiday lets:

You would be liable to pay both UK income and capital gains tax on what you earn from a holiday let in the UK. But you would have to prove that the property is maintained on a commercial basis, and it would be eligible for some tax relief like all businesses (e.g. you can claim cleaning and maintenance costs against income so that if you make £100 but it costs you £10 to replace the light bulbs only £90 is taxable). To be eligible, the property must be:

- *In the UK or the European Economic Area (EEA) which is fast expanding and now includes 30 countries (see Glossary, page 304)*
- *Furnished*
- *Available for letting as a holiday accommodation for at least 140 days a year, or let for a minimum of 70, at the market rental rate – not cheaply – to friends and family*
- *Not let for more than 31 days at one time, and not to the same person in one year*

If you meet all these requirements for 210 days in the year there are no restrictions on longer lets in the remaining 155 days. But longer lets do not count as holiday lets.

You could make further tax savings by taking into account:

- *Loss relief – if after calculating your tax and deducting your expenditure allowances, you incur a loss, you will be entitled to relief. (As explained in Chapter 4.)*
- *Landlord's Energy Saving Allowance (LESA) – as a landlord you can claim a deduction on your taxable income for installing insulation in your holiday let. This also applies to any other property you might be letting.*
- *Pension contributions – any money you put into a pension has the tax you would have paid added in, so for every £80 you put in, another £20 of the tax you would have paid is added to it, if you're a standard-rate taxpayer.*
- *Deducting costs – such as buildings insurance, contents cover if your property is furnished, maintenance costs and the running costs of the property (ground rent, service charges, repairs, letting and management fees, etc.).*

## Buy-to-let properties

Buy-to-let is a form of residential investment where you buy a property, often with the aid of a mortgage, and rent it out. By doing this you become a landlord, and so effectively, for tax purposes, running a small business.

You have to pay tax on the income you get from letting the property but you are allowed to offset against that income certain expenses including:

- *The interest on the mortgage you take out (NB the interest only, you can't offset capital repayments).*
- *Any lettings agency fees.*
- *Maintenance costs, furnishing and decorating costs, or you can just opt for 'wear and tear' which means you can offset 10% of the rental income.*
- *Any cleaning, gardening or other work done at the property (or properties) even if you employ a relative to do it.*
- *You can also claim Landlord's Energy Saving Allowance for the cost of draught-proofing, or insulating the walls, floors, lofts or hot-water systems (up to £1,500 per property).*

## The 'rent a room' scheme

I cannot stress what a great idea this is for home-owners – I'm always banging on about it!

If you have a spare room in your house or flat you could get up to £4,250 tax-free income. The accommodation has to be furnished and a part of the main property you live in. If your rental income is below £4,250, the exemption is automatic, but if it isn't, tell the tax office as you will have to fill out a tax return.

If you usually fill out a tax return then consider whether

you're better off in the scheme or not. Under the scheme you can't claim expenses for wear and tear, insurance, etc., so you may be better off out of the scheme. If you spend more on decorating a room and keeping it in order than you make then you'll be making a loss and not liable for any tax.

If you have made a net profit after all these expenses have been extracted it is added to your other non-savings income and taxed at 20% if you are a normal-rate taxpayer or 40% if you are a higher-rate taxpayer.

However, if you incur losses, they could be offset against future rental profits as well.

## ISAs

I have covered ISAs pretty thoroughly elsewhere in this book so for this section suffice it to say that if you are a taxpayer and over 18 at least some of your investments should be operated through the tax-saving wrapper of an ISA.

The future of ISAs is by no means certain. It is entirely up to different governments as to whether they will continue them and increase or reduce the amount you can put in each year. However, although for the next few years of the twenty-first century consecutive governments are likely to reduce tax benefits in order to claw back some of the billions they lost in the credit crunch, it's unlikely that they will completely do away with the tax incentive to save.

The government knows that it has to encourage us to save more to reduce the future burden on the state of people retiring on almost no personal independent income at all. One in three working Brits doesn't bother with making pension arrangements. The figure is higher for women (40%) than it is for men (33%). Relying on state handouts is a terrible idea, especially as you should really be financing what is in your bucket list of ideas.

It is up to you what kind of an ISA you put your money in but my strong advice is to use it for what it was intended – a tax-saving vehicle for long-term investment – and put it in equities or securities-based products.

Also, if you can, put the money in at the beginning of the tax year to benefit from the full year's worth of growth rather than (as I often do!) waiting until the end of March to make up your mind.

# Capital Gains Tax (CGT)

Capital gains tax (CGT) is paid on investments that we sell at a profit. So that could be shares that have gained in value or a buy-to-let property or a classic painting that has doubled in price since you bought it, for example. It's a nuisance of a tax (aren't they all?) and currently takes out 18% of your 'gains' after your allowance threshold. However, there are a few ways that you can reduce the bill:

- *As with income tax, we all have a CGT allowance each tax year (£10,100 for 2010–11) so you are only taxed on the amount you make in the tax year above that threshold. If you're married or in a civil partnership and you have assets to sell then consider putting some or all in the name of the lower taxpayer in the couple as that will reduce your joint tax bill.*
- *Happily, if you sell share-based investments at a loss – say they*

*have fallen in value but you sell them anyway – you can offset these losses against any gains you have made on other investments in that tax year. So, if you lose £1,000 when you sell some shares, you can add that £1,000 on to your CGT allowance, which will help if you have made gains on other things you have sold in the same year.*

- *Property that you live in – the main family home – doesn't attract any capital gains tax when you sell it, even if it has doubled in value. But if you sell a second property at a profit you pay 18% tax, minus some allowances.*

- *However, selling investment property, including property you have abroad, does attract CGT, although you can offset against your profit any costs you incurred in increasing its value (so that means the cost of building an extension or redeveloping the whole place and, therefore, increasing its value) though not the general, ongoing maintenance that you would claim against the income on the property.*

Remember, folks, it's important to keep records of purchases and sales of assets including stock dividend vouchers, invoices for costs you claim against the purchase, improvement or sale of an asset (e.g. builders' receipts, estate agents' bills, etc., if it's a property), and documents relating to assets you acquired but didn't buy yourself (gifts from relatives perhaps).

# Stamp Duty

You are likely to pay two types of stamp duty during your investment life:

- *Stamp duty land tax*
- *Stamp duty (on shares purchases)*

In both cases stamp duty is paid by the buyer, not the seller. The amount of tax you pay varies depending on the value of the asset you're buying, also in both cases.

Stamp duty land tax is payable when you buy residential property and there are taxable bands for different property prices. Currently they are:

| | |
|---|---|
| Properties worth less than £125,000 | 0% |
| Properties worth between £125,000-250,000 | 1% |
| Properties worth between £250,000-500,000 | 3% |
| Properties worth over £500,000 | 4% |
| (NB New, zero-carbon homes are tax free. Whoopie) | |

With stamp duty on the purchase of shares you pay 0.5% of the value of the shares you are buying. One of the great things about ETFs (exchange-traded funds – see Chapter 4) is that as they are based in Eire there is no stamp duty to pay when you buy them, which makes them even better value.

Other than investing in more ETFs, sadly there's no other way of avoiding stamp duty, either on shares or property. It's a tax you have to pay and just swallow the pain.

# Inheritance Tax (IHT)

This is something you shouldn't need to think about too much until you are past retirement age. Reducing inheritance tax (IHT) is a huge subject and there is more detail to it than is possible to include in this book.

However, although inheritance tax planning is important once you have lived your full three-score years and ten (and I expect much more), one never knows what could happen. So at the very least, as soon as you have any sort of property or investments and certainly as soon as you enter into some kind of long-term relationship or have children, you must make a will. It doesn't matter what age you are, just do it.

More than half of us die 'intestate', that is, without a will. This causes a load of nuisance – and potential expense – to the loved ones who survive us and it means they can lose out on a lot of the money they might have inherited. The tax office loves people who leave no will because that pours billions into the government coffers each year. If you die intestate they take 40% of your worth before anyone else gets a sniff of it.

You can make your own will using a will pack from WHSmith, Tesco or Office World (priced at about £15) or one of the many on the Internet such as Tenminutewill.co.uk or Will-writing-solutions.co.uk. The Co-operative Legal Services, a subsidiary of the Co-operative supermarket, do a standard will for £115, and charge £184 for you and your partner, if you want to make a will together.

A better solution, if you are a 'high net worth' individual (i.e. rich) is to get a solicitor to draw one up for you. Contact the Society of Trust and Estate Practitioners (STEP) for will-writing specialists (Step.org or phone 020 7340 0500).

Or do it for charity. Once a year the Law Society of England and Wales runs a 'Make a Will' week, when solicitors write wills for a one-off donation to charity. Another scheme is Will Aid, where thousands of solicitors donate the fees they make for will-writing to charity for one month. Keep an eye on the media and on Moneymagpie.com for when these events come up this year.

## GENERAL INHERITANCE TAX PLANNING

One useful recent change in inheritance tax laws has meant that married couples and those in a civil partnership can transfer their inheritance tax to a tax-free band. The inheritance tax threshold for 2010–11 is £325,000 so this means that couples could potentially leave £650,000 between them without incurring inheritance tax. The allowance is backdated to October 2007 but it could benefit anyone whose spouse died over the past 35 years or so.

Apart from this nice tax-free bonus, there are a number of things you can do to mitigate the tax burden your inheritors may have to bear (or things your parents could do for you now). As this book is aimed primarily at people who have some years to go before they seriously consider retiring, I will only give you the top-line points to be aware of. There is a plethora of information about the nitty-gritty of IHT planning on the web and several books. Start with the HMRC's website and guides (details at the end of this chapter) and look at books such as *Wills, Probate & Inheritance Tax for Dummies* by Julian Knight. I have suggested a few more on page 319.

Easy ways to avoid some IHT:

- *Make use of all the tax-free gifts you are allowed to make. These are amounts of money that you can give away while you are alive including up to £3,000 per tax year to anyone, up to £5,000 to your child getting married (£2,500 if you're a grandparent, £1,000 if you're anything else), small gifts up to £250 per recipient per year, normal expenditure from your income such as regular payments to an insurance policy for your children.*

- *Any gift of money or goods that you transfer over at least seven years before you die is free of IHT (but, importantly, you must not then benefit from these gifts such as handing over a house that you continue to live in).*

- *Set up trusts that shelter your money from the tax man. You will need specialist help with this from probate lawyers and/or accountants.*

- *Consider taking out a life-insurance policy that would cover the impending tax bill.*

# Don't Let the Tax Tail Wag the Investment Dog

How's that for a financial metaphor?

While we're on the subject of tax and how to avoid it, it's worth mentioning that although it's a very sound fundamental principle to avoid tax where possible – by using your ISA allowance and making the most of your spouse's capital gains tax allowance, for example – don't get carried away.

There are a few investments on the market that are tax free but are still not worth investing in. Make sure that, as the old adage goes, you don't get so hooked on avoiding tax that you invest in the wrong things.

## NATIONAL SAVINGS & INVESTMENTS (NS&I)

### Pros and cons

The government-backed National Savings & Investments (NS&I) came into their own after the collapse of Northern Rock in 2007 and the subsequent stomach-churning lurches all the high-street banks seemed to make towards imminent collapse. Suddenly, NS&I with its generally uninspiring products with small returns looked like the only safe haven in increasingly choppy seas.

The NS&I can be seen as the savings arm of HM Treasury, and this has its perks. Unlike high-street banks that offer a £50,000 compensation limit (i.e. if the bank collapses then the government guarantees the first £50k of your savings with that banking group), if they have the right licensing, the NS&I guarantees all your capital – no matter how much you invest. However, this safety brings with it generally very low returns. Even with the tax saving, most of their products will give you little to smile about.

## PREMIUM BONDS

I can guarantee that every single money workshop I do there will be someone who puts up their hand and says 'But what about premium bonds? Aren't they a good investment? They're tax free' and my heart sinks.

Yes, they're tax free but the average return, even with the tax saving, is about the same as you get with average savings accounts. As one who is staunchly opposed to gambling in all its forms (I don't even buy raffle tickets), I never see the point anyway. However, if you love to have a flutter and if putting a bit of cash into premium bonds would stop you sticking it on the 3.30 at Chepstow, then go ahead!

## VENTURE CAPITAL TRUSTS (VCTs) AND THE ENTERPRISE INVESTMENT SCHEMES (EIS)

As I will describe in Chapter 10, these are typically small investment trusts that have so far had generally unimpressive records in their short lives. Even with the substantial tax breaks that come with them, the net returns have been so poor as to make you wonder why anyone has bothered.

Part of the problem is the very high fees they charge investors and the other part (in my opinion) is that so many of them are simply run very badly. I have a number of friends and contacts who have had money invested in their companies by VCTs, for example, who say that they would never touch them again.

The carrot to invest in them is the tax breaks. With VCTs you get income tax relief at 30% up to a maximum investment of £200,000 per tax year. You have to keep your shares (VCTs are companies that are listed on the stock exchange and you invest by buying shares) for at least five years. You do not have to pay tax on dividends (although you still have the 10% tax credit which cannot be reclaimed) and any profit on shares is free of capital gains. However, you can't claim relief on any losses.

With the EIS you get tax relief of 20% of the amount you pay for shares up to a maximum of £500,000. You have to keep the shares for a minimum of three years. Any gain you make on the shares is free of capital gains tax (so long as you have kept them for at least three years). Also if the company fails and you lose on your shares you can claim tax relief on the amount of your loss minus the amount you saved when you bought the shares. You can either offset the loss against your taxable income for the year of the loss (or the year before) or against your capital gains.

These are a highly 'risky' investment with a poor history. They are also relatively illiquid as you are required to keep the shares for a few years so you can't jump out when you see yourself losing. As far as I am concerned, until I see a good five years' worth of more impressive performance I certainly won't bother with either of them – tax break or not.

## Where to Go for Up-To-Date Help

One of the joys of taxation is that it keeps changing as each Chancellor brings in new rules. Things will also change for you as your circumstances alter and the amount you make increases or decreases.

Happily the tax office (Her Majesty's Revenue & Customs, HMRC, as it's now known) has a wide range of websites and helplines to give you free help. If you have a good tax accountant you will also get help from them, although it will cost. It's worth trying the free route first and then just filling in the gaps with your accountant.

## WEBSITES

| | |
|---|---|
| HMRC website | www.hmrc.gov.uk |
| Capital gains manual | www.hmrc.gov.uk/manuals/cg1manual |
| Enterprise Investment Scheme | www.hmrc.gov.uk/eis/ |
| How to pay a tax bill | www.hmrc.gov.uk/howtopay/index.htm |
| Inheritance tax customer guide | ww.hmrc.gov.uk/cto/iht.htm |
| Property income manual | www.hmrc.gov.uk/manuals/pimmanual |
| Self-assessment | www.hmrc.gov.uk/sa/index.htm |
| Trusts | www.hmrc.gov.uk/trusts |
| Venture Capital Trusts | www.hmrc.gov.uk/guidance/vct.htm |
| Directgov (your answers to life, the universe and everything, including financial info) | www.direct.gov.uk |

## HELPLINES

| | |
|---|---|
| Probate and inheritance tax | 0845 302 0900 |
| Self-assessment | 0845 900 0444 |
| Shares and assets valuation | 0115 974 2222 |
| Stamp duty | 0845 603 0135 |
| Taxation of bank and building society interest | 0845 980 0645 |

## Chapter 9
# Odds and Ends

So we've gone through the main types of investments that you should be considering for your diversified portfolio – cash, shares, property, bonds and pensions – but of course that's not the end of the story. There are many and varied other types of investments, mixed funds (including some shares, some bonds, some cash, etc.) and new and different investment ideas coming out all the time.

In this chapter I'm going to go into more detail than I have in my previous books on covering three of the main alternative investments that have become popular in recent years – investments that you might already have or you're thinking of getting into:

**Gold:**  a commodity that is always popular, particularly in times of economic uncertainty.
**Collections:**  increasingly viewed as a serious asset class, even if you collect daft, kitsch stuff.

**Ethical investments:** these could go in the 'Shares' chapter but many people who wouldn't normally bother with shares are interested in ethical products.

# Investing in Gold

*Skill level: beginner to advanced*

*Risk level: low to medium*

The human race has had a love affair with gold for millennia. It's probably the colour, as well as its utility and rarity, that has made it so valuable for so long. In many ways it's odd that it has continued to be so prized as it's not the rarest or the most useful metal in the world. However, it has had (and in some places still has) a mythical status in our collective thinking and it shows no signs of dropping off in value any time soon. In fact, the more uncertain the times get and the rockier economies look, the more people rush to the haven of gold.

In fact, seasoned gold investors like it when other markets fall as this is typically when the price of gold starts to rise. And if the price of gold falls in the short term, the chances are it will climb again in time because of its inherent perceived value.

If you love the idea of investing in gold in some way then you can consider it a pretty safe haven for up to 15% of your cash. It's also worth noting that since gold is in relatively short supply – mining output peaked in 2003 – it can be sold fairly quickly should you want to cash it in.

However, be aware that gold is valued in dollars on the markets, so even if the value of gold rises, British sellers can lose out should the pound be weak. Yet even when this is the case, gold can still be a decent investment if the market conditions are good (in other words – conditions are bad for other forms of investment). The economic aftershocks of the credit crunch look set to be with us for a while yet, which means that investors are likely to continue to back 'safe bets' like gold.

So if you feel that investing in gold is an option you'd like to explore, there are several ways you can do this including:

- *Buying bullion*
- *Gold exchange-traded funds*
- *Gold stocks*
- *Gold futures*

## BULLION

*Skill level: beginner*

Bullion can be bought in several forms including gold bars, coins or jewellery. After all, a stock-market crash is a bit easier to endure with the knowledge that you have some coins lying snugly in a safe that are likely to gain in value gently!

These days you can buy gold from online dealers like Bullionvault.com. For a full list of reputable dealers, try the World Gold Council (Gold.org). Click on 'Investment' and then 'Where to Invest', which will take you to their full gold-buying directory. The London Bullion Market Association also has a members' list on their website (Lbma.org.uk).

Small bars and bullion coins can be bought from dealers such as Spink.com, at about 5% above metal value and sold back at the same rate below value. Metal value, by the way, is the value of a coin only in terms of the pure, base metal the coin is composed of. Dealers make it cheaper for customers who buy or sell in bulk.

The amount 'bulk' is depends on the dealer, and how much you're buying. It's often down to the discretion of the dealer or your haggling skills! However, some stores, like the American Gold Exchange, offer a structured 'the more you buy, less you pay' incentive. See their website (Amergold.com) for some pricing examples.

British gold coins (known as 'sovereigns' because they portray the reigning monarch) are especially attractive because they weigh a quarter of an ounce, and were the original pound coin. This also means that they are not subject to capital gains tax, because they still count as currency. So when you sell them you gain the full amount. Also, gold bullion and older gold coins are not subject to VAT, due to the EU Gold Directive.

New coins are priced according to their weight, but older coins can have a higher collectors' value. But if you are intending to buy coins with a 'collectable' value then be prepared to do a heck of a lot of research to be able to spot what's valuable and what's a rip-off – plain gold investments might be for beginners but gold collectables are for the advanced gold specialist investor.

If you don't want to keep gold at home because of the risk of theft, you could use a safe-deposit box offered by many providers for a monthly, quarterly or annual fee. You can choose to keep the key to the box, and access the contents by arrangement, and remove or replace items as you wish. You can look up where these facilities are available in your area in the Yellow Pages under 'safes and vaults'. Most banks also offer this service.

It's important to remember that if you need cash urgently, it may take a bit of luck finding a buyer for your gold at short notice. One way to get round this is to buy gold through an online dealer like BullionVault.com. BullionVault holds its gold in 400-ounce bars, at secure vaults in Zurich, London and New York, but you can buy in units of just one gram. So there is no gold bar with your name on it – just an audited amount of gold in the dealer's coffer. You'll get a pretty good price as this way you don't have to pay the kind of premiums that come with coins and small bars. Underlying this is the promise that should you decide to sell it, they give you your money back.

Of course, there is a commission charge. But 0.8% is competitive – when buying coins and small bars for private custody, the costs are approximately 6%, insurance is expensive and finding buyers willing to trust you can be difficult. Plus, with BullionVault you can buy gold in a variety of amounts from as small as 1 gram to as large as 1 kilogram and beyond. BullionVault storage charge is 0.12% per annum (compared to around 1.25% a bank would charge).

### Can I expect a decent return on my investment?

Gold's value climbed 140% between 2004 and 2009, though it has only shown a modest increase of a few per cent in the 12 months to December 2009. Gold is a natural hedge against inflation and currency volatility, and is often used more as a bedrock of wealth preservation rather than an investment that's expected to turn a massive profit. Gold isn't immune to price slumps, but long term it's a pretty safe bet. If you buy at the right time – in other words, when other asset classes are doing well and gold is, therefore, cheap – it can prove to be a shrewd investment. However, as with other investments, if everyone else is buying then it's probably not a good idea to follow suit as the price will be high.

## Who should invest in bullion?

It's a suitable option for most people who are looking to diversify their investment portfolio, although initial dealing costs for buying basic gold are high – sometimes 5% or even higher every time you buy or sell. It's best to stick to ordinary bullion in gold coins, or if you want to make a massive investment, bars. A non-collectable gold coin costs a few hundred pounds – often more than its metal weight. A gold bar costs several thousand pounds so in many cases ordinary gold coins are the most accessible and simple form of gold bullion purchase. Keep that in mind.

## JEWELLERY

*Skill level: advanced*

Many people confuse the cost of buying jewellery as a consumer good with its value as an investment. Unfortunately, the notion that buying jewellery is a good investment in and of itself is a bit of an old wives' tale.

Jewellery is a luxury item and can drop in value by around 50% as soon as you've bought it. It's rather like buying a new car. Concealed in the price of jewellery is the rent that the dealer would be paying for a high-street shop, the shop's staff, the dealer's insurance costs, VAT and so on. Also, jewellery can never be more than 24 carat gold, as it would be too soft to be durable, so the value of the actual gold in it is not as high as you should aim for in an investment.

Besides, if you wore it, there might be repair and maintenance costs – and what would be the fun of owning jewellery if you couldn't wear it and had to put it away in a safe instead?

### Can I expect a decent return on my investment?

If you've managed to pick up a rare antique piece, then probably. Otherwise, jewellery is subject to such high mark-ups that it's not really a suitable investment choice.

### Who should invest in jewellery?

Expert antiques dealers and collectors.

## GOLD EXCHANGE-TRADED FUNDS

*Skill level: intermediate*

A great way to invest in gold is through exchange-traded funds (ETFs). As I have mentioned a few times already in other chapters, these can be bought and sold on the stock market like ordinary shares. They're cheap, easy to buy and sell, and can be held tax free in an ISA or SIPP. Unlike conventional shares, no stamp duty applies to ETFs.

ETFs track the price of gold. It's a quick and effective way of moving money in or out of the market. (If you already have a broking account, there is no need to set a new arrangement. If not, see page 317 for a list of online brokers to join.) You can follow the progress of your fund in the mainstream financial press such as the *Financial Times*, or on Teletext, and of course on the Internet – just as you might follow any other stock.

ETFs aren't managed by a fund manager. They are 'passive' funds, and so are less expensive. There aren't any management fees to pay, just a small annual administration charge (typically around 0.4% and 0.5% – much lower than the 1.5% average that a typical unit trust would charge).

A gold ETF is regarded as a safe option. ETFS Physical Gold and ETFS Gold Bullion Securities are examples of gold funds you could consider as long-term investments. Of course, the price of gold can certainly go down as well as up – but in the long term, gold tends to retain its value and always does well in times of economic uncertainty.

### Can I expect a decent return on my investment?
ETFs are a cost-effective way to broaden your investment portfolio, but to get any real benefit you will probably have to invest for the long term – we're talking five years or more.

Derivative-based funds can offer more short-term, eye-catching rewards – but you should be extremely cautious if investing in these as the risks are much greater.

### Who should invest in ETFs?
Those who want a simple, cheap and hassle-free way of investing in the stock market. They're extremely flexible (so if you want to pull your money out at short notice, you can) but their low charges make them a good long-term option.

## GOLD STOCKS
*Skill level: advanced*

Gold stocks are not actually gold (obviously!), and are more of a speculative investment than investing directly in the shiny stuff itself. If you're looking for more of a safe bet, you're probably better off going for one of the other investment options.

Investing in gold stocks is, in fact, stock-picking in the gold sector. Stock-picking is covered in Chapter 4 in more detail, but the long and short of it is that you have to be dedicated to finding out a great deal about the gold-mining companies before you buy any shares.

You could go for a managed fund and let them do all the research for you, but as I've said before, expect high fees for this 'help'. One such fund, the BlackRock Merrill Lynch Gold Fund, has performed outstandingly well since 1988, but who's to say that it can continue that performance in the future?

Here's something that's rarely considered: I recommend that investments are for 'a richer life' in all senses and another issue to take into account is the ethics of gold-mining operations. Some gold-mining outfits displace local communities and even use child labour. The large-scale formal mining community is far more regulated, but it can be hard to determine just how ethically sourced the gold you're investing in is. Gold mining can also be extremely environmentally damaging. Do a little research, because it's always better to feel good about your investments. No amount of riches will clear your conscience! (For investing ethically see also page 265.)

### Can I expect a decent return on my investment?

Only if you are prepared to study this sector in detail and invest in what you consider to be a good company with a good future.

### Who should invest in gold stocks?
Dedicated investors who are prepared to study the market.

## GOLD FUTURES

*Skill level: Warren Buffett*

These are high-risk investments in which experts are attempting to predict how the value of gold will change in the short term. Don't go there!

### Can I expect a decent return on my investment?
Not unless you are a serious investor.

### Who should invest in gold stocks?
Wealthy risk takers who have an in-depth knowledge of the gold market.

# Collecting

*Skill level: medium to hard*

*Risk level: medium to high*

Collections of every variety have always been popular, and for many, a wonderfully satisfying and sometimes eccentric hobby. And that is what you have to be if you are going to make any money on this – a dedicated hobbyist. That's the only way you are going to be able to tell the difference between an undervalued treasure and a piece of tat.

What's worse, since SIPP rules were modified in 2006, only more conventional investments in shares, unit trusts, commercial property and other established asset classes can now be included in a SIPP – collections of cars, jewellery, paintings and wine cannot.

## WHAT SHOULD I COLLECT?

Whatever you like. Literally.

The best aspect and most essential requirement of investing in a collection is that you buy what you know and love. In all likelihood the biggest return on such an investment will be having around you those things that you love. If you make money on them as well, that's a big bonus.

The great thing about collecting is that just about anything is collectable. Here are some of the most popular collections that trade between enthusiasts today: antiquarian books, antiques, art deco, autographs, barometers, Beanie Babies, Barbie dolls, buttons, cameras, china, clocks, comics, corkscrews, Disneyana, dolls, fossils, jewellery, keys, knives, lace, maps and charts, model soldiers, newspapers, paperweights, perfume bottles, phone cards, Pokemon, posters, rocks, royal memorabilia, rugs, sci-fi memorabilia, silver shells, snuff boxes, stamps, teddy bears, tools, typewriters, weapons, writing accessories . . .

In fact the list is almost endless and seems to be growing all the time. As technology advances, even prosaic items like the early mobile phones, Betamax tape recorders and early home computers have sometimes shot up in value.

> A case in point is early technology, which has sold very well over the years. People who have collected working television sets from the 1940s and 1950s have not only done well at auction but are able to hire their old televisions out as props in period dramas. But again the return on this 'investment' is mostly sentimental.

Collecting experts say that if you want to buy things that are likely to be valuable in 10 or 20 years' time you should invest in items that today's teenage boys want but can't afford. This is why BMX and chopper bikes have become collectables recently. So iPhones, Xboxes and top-of-the-range trainers (in pristine condition of course and, ideally, in their boxes) are worth considering for future profit.

## HOW DO I START A COLLECTION?

Firstly ask yourself what items you find fascinating – you'll need that passion to drive you to do the endless research necessary. Unless you have the money to invest in the larger ticket items, like fine wines, antiquarian books or classic cars, it makes sense to collect something more affordable. That could be comic books, watercolours or barometers – things that will enrich your life even if they might never pay for a luxury holiday or a new wardrobe.

## WILL I MAKE MONEY?

Assume that you won't, then you may be surprised!

If you speak to most dedicated philatelists (serious stamp collectors), they are enthused about the story behind each individual stamp – where it was posted to and from, what the political intrigues were behind the designs. Their enthusiasm and dedication mean that they have an asset of very last resort that they can sell if they absolutely have to, but that's not why they collect. Nor should you.

However, there are some rules to follow if you would like to make money out of the things you love.

Rarity – generally, the rarer things are, the more valuable, although that doesn't always hold true. The market ensures that rarity of any object increases the value, so the fewer the better as far as a collector is concerned. For example, at the top end of valuable collections are books printed before 1500, which are both rare and precious. And don't forget seemingly ordinary objects such as light bulbs, which can be worth thousands of pounds – if they were one of the first light bulbs, produced by Thomas Edison himself. More romantically, the few hundred Stradivarius violins made in the eighteenth century now attract millions of dollars at auction. Consortiums of music lovers sometimes invest in antique instruments because of both their passion and the fact these are investments which have so far only increased in value.

But don't despair if you have only started collecting recently. Rarity is not necessarily determined by age. One of the most valuable stamps on offer only dates from 2004. It is a two-dollar New Zealand stamp that celebrates the Olympics. That sounds very ordinary until you learn that the image of a runner was printed upside-down on a tiny number of these stamps. In fact only 30 of these misprints have been reported and they are currently changing hands for around £2,000.

Then there are other items that are relatively old, like postage stamps from the early twentieth century, which seem like they should be valuable. But remember that 100 years ago everyone wrote letters all the time. In fact it was the only way to communicate unless you and the other person possessed a rare phone, sent an expensive telegram or met face to face. It was quite a different world before texting and emails. Consequently postage stamps were produced in the millions and millions. So those stamp collections started by your great-uncle may be beautiful to view, but perhaps not quite as valuable as you might hope.

Condition – the quality of that article is very important for most collectables. Some things (such as an electric guitar that was smashed on stage by Pete Townsend of The Who) increase their value with wear, but the majority will only bring in really good money if they are in great condition.

Sadly, collectable toys and memorabilia (like Barbies, Beanie Babies, Elvis dolls, action figures, etc.) tend to be more valuable if they are still in their boxes and have never been played with. It seems pointless to me to buy a toy and then refuse to play with it, but for many collectors it's the thing itself that is of value, not, generally, the playing with it!

Designer clothes are increasingly bought as investments and, again, need to be kept in good condition to bring in a good profit when sold. I have a friend who paid for an extension on her house by selling her collection of Vivienne Westwood clothes from the 1970s. However, she has always known a lot about fashion and kept the clothes in wonderful condition, storing them in tissue paper, having them dry-cleaned and wearing them (if she wore them at all) carefully.

Popularity – this last factor is down to simple sheer luck or perhaps a good crystal ball – if you found one of those in your attic clean-out. It can make all the difference between your collection funding your retirement and simply sitting there collecting dust for the rest of your life. Other contemporary collectables, like fine art, often increase in value after the death of the artists. For a quick illustration of this, go to art auctions of modern paintings and watch how the bidding can increase for the work of artists well over pensionable age.

What will be fashionable in the future is the most problematic area for collectors. Being able to predict what people will want to buy in the coming years is a real skill. Get this right and you can do well.

One good example is in the art world. Less than 20 years ago many Indian miniatures – the delicate eighteenth- and nineteenth-century paintings from the Indian subcontinent – could be purchased for very modest prices by travellers in India or collectors in Europe. But suddenly both Western collectors and Indian citizens sought out these delightful pictures. Why? Partly it was because the Indian economy had grown and prospered and Indians with a greater disposable income had seized the chance to celebrate their heritage, and partly because the art market had expanded so more people learnt about the miniatures and were captivated by them. Within a few years the prices of these charming pictures shot up to four- and five-figure numbers. It was a similar story for Chinese art and ceramics, driven to a great extent by newly wealthy Chinese business people with a love of their cultural history.

Other fashionable collectables have surprised experts who felt that mass-produced items might only have a novelty value. But there is an indefinable emotional element in some collections. Beanie Babies, for example, were first marketed in 1993 costing only a few pounds each. But they crucially managed to appeal to both children and adults. Within a few years Beanie Babies were the number one toy in America and hugely popular worldwide.

This was helped by having been marketed carefully. Only about a dozen new Beanie designs are introduced every year and each year the same number is usually 'retired' to help promote the rarity value. So far, the fashion for Beanies has held and the early designs can be worth up to £1,000. It helps, by the way, that these are particularly popular in America. Items that are sought after by Americans – given that there are so many of them, relative to Brits – often grow in value much faster simply because of the massive increase in demand.

On the downside, some items seem clearly destined to go down in value. Some stamp experts, for example, believe that the demand for stamps – and their value – might well decrease in another few decades. This is simply because stamp collecting is now considered a slightly old-fashioned interest. One dealer pointed out to me that the average age of the serious collectors that he knew was over 60. And not many young collectors are emerging. So perhaps in another generation, the interest and demand for stamps may start to dwindle along with their value.

Demographic data can be a sort of guide to what people may want in coming years, but predicting the future demand for most things can simply come down to speculation.

## HOW DO I FIND OUT THE VALUE OF MY COLLECTION?

Whether you are collecting stuffed toys or musical instruments, it's always fascinating to find out what they're really worth. For some items, there are professionals who will value your collection, usually for free or sometimes for a small fee.

Stamps and autographs can be valued and appraised at Stanley Gibbons, for example. Auction houses like Bonhams (Bonhams.com) regularly value antique dolls, rocking horses and teddy bears and other collectables. In fact, auction houses of all kinds usually publish their catalogues online as well as guides on how to buy and sell. And don't forget museums, which have collections of fans, scientific instruments or costumes and textiles. Visit them or get in touch with their curators. Many of them welcome visitors who want an expert to view their more modest offerings. Sometimes they won't even charge because they are simply so interested in the items. You could even take a trip to the *Antiques Roadshow* and get one of the celebrity dealers to evaluate your items!

If your collection does not fall into an obvious category, a little time spent surfing websites might well give you a good indication of prices and valuations. Websites such as Collectorcafe.com, Collectibles.about.com and Antiqueswebsite.co.uk cover a wide range of collections. Sites like Valuemystuffnow.com will even offer you instant valuations for a small fee. Do a bit of online research and you can find valuations for just about anything. Even going on eBay and searching for something that is as close as possible to what you have will give you an idea of what people are willing to pay for it right now.

If you are thinking of selling, Internet research is a good way to also find out where the kind of people who want to collect your favourite things can be found. And there is an amazing number of collector clubs online which can provide good tips on acquiring, maintaining and selling collections. And check out other quirkier online sales sites like Bonanzle.com.

## COSTS

When working out how much you could make on a collection, don't forget to factor in the costs of amassing this stuff. Potential costs include:

Insurance – particularly important for art, antiques and items where the value is generally known. Many collectors recommend getting a current market valuation from an expert and updating this every few years. You will need to talk to your home contents insurance company about insuring individual items. This can add £100s, even £1,000s to your annual policy.

Repair, cleaning and maintenance – again, for very valuable items this can be quite substantial.

Storage – it's worth keeping this in mind if you are undecided as to what to collect. For example, coins or antique jewellery are easier and cheaper to store (in your drawers or cupboards) than, say, vintage cars.

Buying and selling – if you buy through eBay or Sotheby's you are going to be charged commission and then again when you sell. If you sell to shops or antique stalls you will sell at a lower price than they think they could sell for. All these costs should be taken into account.

Tax – if you make a profit on your collection when you sell some or all of it you will be liable to capital gains tax on any profit you make over and above the current threshold for this tax year. Factor that in to your calculations too. (See Chapter 8 for more explanation on tax and filling in your self-assessment form )

# Ethical Investing

*Skill level: intermediate to advanced*

*Risk level: medium to high*

## WHAT IS ETHICAL INVESTING?

Ethical investing or Socially Responsible Investment (SRI) is generally regarded to have started in the eighteenth century when the Quakers made a moral stand and refused to invest in any company which supported the slave trade. This method of choosing investments based on an ethical stance rather than on financial gain has increased in popularity over recent decades.

Friends Provident launched the first ethically screened investment fund in the UK in 1985. They promised not to invest in armaments, alcohol, tobacco or oppressive governments. Today in the UK around £7 billion is invested in ethical funds, which have a very wide range of investment criteria. These funds now offer nearly 100 different investment products to choose from for ethical financial return.

## WHAT IS AN ETHICAL FUND?

There are two different ways in which ethical funds base their choices:

- *Negative criteria – some will screen out companies that include what they consider to be negative practices (producing tobacco products, pornography, alcohol, arms, for example).*
- *Positive criteria – these funds are based on investing in companies that promote green solutions to energy or human rights or many more factors that might be considered to promote and create social good.*

Some investors have made decisions not to invest in a company that is regarded as cooperating with certain governments. For example, companies that had dealings with the regimes of Saddam Hussein, Robert Mugabe or the military government of Burma were 'screened out' by some investors.

Another method used by some investors and fund managers is to actively monitor and divest – i.e. remove stocks – from their portfolio based on ethical reasons. This allows an opportunity to monitor changing conditions in different industries or countries. Many churches are known to continually reassess their investments in this way and ensure that they continue to meet their particular ethical standards.

But you can do more than simply 'screen out' investments which you might object to on moral and ethical grounds. Some ethical investors actively 'screen in' investments which they want to support.

The question of 'screening in' or positive screening can be a vexing issue. This is the stage where you have to make some probing decisions on certain criteria: what do you believe is responsible investing for a positive social impact? These investments could include supporting companies that promote social justice, minimise impact on the environment and support organic foods and fair-trade producers.

Some funds are built around specific themes such as renewable and alternative energy. A 'green tech' fund like this might invest in solar energy, wind farms, carbon-offsetting, water and waste management. But be aware that these investments could be with companies that are also involved in industries that some ethical funds might screen out.

Other ethical funds include mining companies, multi-national banks and oil and gas companies that are considered to be the 'best in their class' i.e. are working towards a better record on environmental impact. So always do your research before you invest.

The criteria for each ethical fund are necessarily subjective. And these criteria become more complex when you consider the consumer choices you make every day. For example, if you like a glass of wine with dinner, do you screen out alcohol? If you are concerned about animal welfare, do you choose your cosmetics on that basis as well as the companies you invest in? If you are a vegetarian, do you screen out companies that produce or market meat products?

There are any number of variations when it comes to ethical funds. Recently there has been a growth in Shariah funds, which are based on Islamic beliefs. Shariah funds avoid investments in areas regarded as non-Islamic including gambling, tobacco and alcohol. And because the Koran – the holy book of Islam – prohibits charging interest, a Shariah fund would not invest in many of the multinational banks. Both Muslims and non-Muslims can and do invest in these funds. Since the credit crunch they have become even more popular with consumers.

## DOES ETHICAL INVESTING LEAD TO A BETTER WORLD?

Ethical investors want to benefit the world as well as their own finances. Some activists believe that investors can have a substantial effect on influencing governments, companies and individuals on political issues, human rights and environmental actions by investing positively in ethical companies and/or shunning what are perceived as unethical ones.

Some ethical fund investors and managers actively engage or work with companies on improving social or environmental practices. This can take the form of advocacy by participating in shareholder meetings or even consulting with management. Shareholder activism has positively influenced corporate behaviour and encouraged companies to consider issues such as workers' conditions, environmental impact and relations with foreign governments.

In the end, it can be very difficult to measure the effect of ethical investment other than by looking at specific cases. However, I do believe that it is much easier to influence a company if you are an active shareholder, particularly if you are rich enough to have substantial holdings, than if you stand outside, throwing rocks!

# HOW TO FIND ETHICAL INVESTMENTS

Like other investments in the stock market, you can choose to invest in individual companies or in managed funds (see Chapter 4 for information on the best ways to go about investing in individual companies and funds). Either way, you will want to research the companies that will be in your portfolio. This information is largely available. So be prepared to spend time reading company and news reports on the Internet. In addition to your own research you can find an ethical financial adviser (IFA) to choose these companies and investments for you. A list of these can be found on Yourethicalmoney.org. Don't forget to find out the details of the cost of investing in a managed fund.

More information is available from the Ethical Investment Association. The EIA was started by financial advisers in 1998 dedicated to sustainable investment in the environment, fair trade and human rights in the UK. The EIA supports advisers who want to offer green and ethical investment advice to their clients: Ethicalinvestment.org.uk.

The FTSE – the Financial Times Stock Exchange – offers many different indices including the Responsible Investment Indices. These are known as the FTSE4Good and Environmental Market Index and were launched in 2001.

Each of these has been designed to measure the performance of companies that meet globally recognised corporate responsibility and transparent management standards. The criteria of these standards are listed on their website. Many ethical investment funds use this index to facilitate investments and create what they call 'Responsible Investment Products': www.ftse.com/Indices/FTSE4Good_Index_Series/index.jsp.

The Ethical Investment Research Service provides a good overall view of the criteria that helps determine ethical investment. The EIRIS employs a team of researchers to watch companies, buyouts and takeovers with a view to monitoring their performance of environmental, social, governance (ESG) ethics. The mission statement of the EIRIS is to 'empower responsible investors with independent assessments of companies and advice on integrating them with investment decisions'. This website also lists specific companies given a Transparency Award for their commitment to transparency on green and ethical issues: Eiris.org.

Another useful website for a global view, Enpri.org discusses the principles set by the United Nations for responsible investment.

Finally, if you have investments already, don't forget to ask your current provider if they have an ethical alternative.

## ETHICAL CASH ISAs

Like other investment products, you can choose a cash ISA rather than a fund. These products are marketed as ethical cash ISAs:

- *Ecology.co.uk*
- *Co-operativebank.co.uk*
- *Triodos.co.uk*

### Can I expect a decent return on my investment?

Because there are so many different types of ethical funds, there is no one way to measure their performance. And like many investments since late 2008, it has been a challenging time for ethical investments as well.

It is important to remember that ethical funds are chosen on non-financial reasons. Some financial advisers say that investments should simply be chosen entirely on profitability. Many of the sectors which have been highly profitable like mining, oil and commodities are the sectors which are shunned by many ethical funds. Some financial advisers say the stricter your criteria in determining what is ethical, the more companies you will rule out. But ethical funds have the ability to do just as well as other funds.

Some financial commentators point out that our priorities have been changing towards a greater awareness of ethics In many societies. For example, the World Trade Organisation (WTO) has taken a tough stand on companies who have negative press or fines for exploiting the environment or vulnerable people. Companies with ethical principles may find themselves in stronger market positions and may be among the top financial performers in coming years.

Will companies that value human rights be rewarded in the marketplace? Will the increased interest in carbon neutral products such as solar panels and wind farms improve profits in green investments in the future? As always, opinion is divided and there is a fairly even split on predictions for the performance of ethical funds in the future.

## Who should invest?

First and foremost a person who wants to support and encourage socially responsible practices. If you have strong views on the environment and social issues, ethical investing may be an attractive way to promote your beliefs.

Ethical investing is a very satisfying option if you are

looking to diversify your investment portfolio and want the ethical 'return'. As usual with stock-market investments it's particularly good if you're able and willing to keep your money in for many years.

There are many sound reasons for believing that the ethical sector as a whole will do well in the long term. Transparency of business practices and the ethical treatment of people and animals is increasingly demanded, at least in developed countries. Also, as global warming does its thing across the globe, services such as clean water and proper waste management will become more and more important and, therefore, lucrative.

However, when it comes to individual companies and individual funds, if you're in the business of making money, you need to follow the rules I covered in Chapter 4. The same principles apply. You need to be prepared to do a good amount of research in what you want to invest in and to keep an eye on the companies that you have invested in.

> **What they want you to do:** leave the investment decisions to others and let them invest in a mix of funds and products for you.
>
> **What you should do:** do it yourself. Pick 'n' mix your own investments including collections that you love, a bit of gold, some shares, bonds, property and pensions. DIY mix 'n' match tends to be better and more profitable for you.

There are various other things you could invest in as well as the ideas above. There are many other commodities other than gold, for example, and substances such as iron, steel and zinc do very well when the global economy is booming. You could even find yourself investing in individual businesses too. Once you've set up a good investment bedrock of pensions, shares, bonds and maybe property, there's a whole list of possibilities for you. However, be careful with whatever you invest in. There are many products out there that won't make money for you and will even lose in the short or long term. Look at the next chapter for a list of some that I love to hate.

## Chapter 10

# Products to Avoid

> **What they want you to do:** invest in any of these products and make money for the managers.
>
> **What you should do:** avoid them and go for simpler, cheaper products that make money for you.

Throughout this book I've pointed out ways in which banks try to make a profit out of you rather than for you. In each section I've shown you which versions are likely to give the largest part of the profits to you rather than the banks.

However, there are some products that just have 'BAD' written all over them. And guess what – they're the ones that keep being pushed in adverts on TV, in newspapers and on posters!

Oh yes, if you go to a bank, an adviser, a broker you can bet your bright little buttons they'll try to sell you one or more of the pointless products in this chapter. You don't need to spend much time reading the ins and outs of them. Just get the general idea from this chapter and then you'll be able to discern truly appalling products when they try to sell them to you.

# Life Insurance Products with an Investment Element

## THE GOOD STUFF

If you have children or other dependants it's important that you have life insurance. It's there to make sure that they are provided for if you should die. If you are employed and life insurance is part of your pay package then you may not need to get your own, but if you have a family you should make sure that they are covered one way or another.

There are two main types of life insurance:

- *Term insurance*
- *Whole-of-life insurance*

Term insurance (also sometimes referred to as term assurance) only pays out if you die within a certain term, whereas whole-of-life insurance pays out whenever you die.

## THE BAD STUFF

However, some life-insurance policies contain an investment element, which enables you to invest in the stock market while providing protection for your loved ones. Sounds convenient?

Don't be fooled. These policies tend to cost a lot more than protection-only insurance and the investment portion is generally not good value for money.

You see, the insurance industry worked out a long time ago that they could make more money for themselves if they created products that mixed investment and insurance. With investment-type life insurance, you typically contribute monthly to a policy. Some of these policies only release their money when you die. Others pay out a cash amount on a specified date. The amount paid out by investment-type policies depends on how well the investments linked to the insurance fund have done.

Actually when you think about it, it really is a daft idea. Why bother? Why not just get an insurance policy and invest in the stock market separately? Quite.

If you want to invest, set up an investment through shares, bonds, property or something that is focused on getting you a return for you on your investment. If you want life insurance then get a term policy. Don't mix the two.

## Don't get sucked in by the 'extras'!

Life-insurance policies with an investment element may also offer extra features – things like critical illness cover.

Critical illness cover is a late-twentieth-century luxury thought up by the insurance companies. Most people never consider it or regret not having it.

However, if you are self-employed and the sole or main earner in a household – and you can afford the monthly commitment – it might be worth considering this type of cover for a few key years (particularly while your family is growing and needs to be supported), for peace of mind if nothing else. The cash can be a lifesaver if the policyholder has unexpected health issues that affect their work. Generally speaking these policies will have all sorts of caveats in the small print, e.g. you are not covered for any ailment that you knew about when you applied for the policy – whether or not you declare it. They don't want people who are actually going to get ill, oh no, they just require your money, thanks.

But you don't need an investment life-insurance policy to get it – if it's important to you, be sure to shop around (check out the Moneymagpie.com insurance comparison pages for a start at www.moneymagpie.com/comparisons).

> **What they want you to do:** invest in this rubbish!
> **What you should do:** shop around for the best value life-insurance policy and invest in products and asset types that you've learnt about in other chapters of this book. Don't get sucked in by their marketing materials!

# With-Profits Policies

## WHAT'S SUPPOSED TO HAPPEN

With-profits policies are a form of pooled investment fund, made up of the money invested by all its policyholders. Such policies normally include life cover, but how their funds are used will vary depending on the policy – they invest in everything from bonds to property.

They are essentially managed funds and therefore are generally badly run and involve all sorts of fees, which are usually hidden. They are also quite opaque in the way they are run and what they invest in. If you try to dissect the funds you will find yourself in murky waters with very few precise answers to your questions.

They're mainly aimed at investors who want to make a cautious entry into the stock market without, they think, exposing themselves to too much risk. The companies that market these play on people's fear of the stock market but their desire to benefit from the good years.

A key part of their appeal is the apparent promise of bonuses, which is a major way to increase investment growth. Depending on the policy, bonuses are supposed to be paid annually or at the end of the agreement. But how big a bonus you get is subject to how well the fund's investments have performed. In return for monthly payments, investors are also guaranteed a lump sum at the end of the term of the policy.

Fund profits aren't simply shared out at the end of each year, though. Instead, with-profits policies use a method called 'smoothing'. This is where some of the profits from a successful year are held back, which are then used to top up bonuses when economic times are harder.

## WHAT ACTUALLY HAPPENS

The famed 'bonuses' that are heavily sold as a big reason to invest in these products often simply don't appear. If there is a poor performance year after year – and these are managed funds, remember, so their performance is more than likely to be poor – then you don't see any extras.

With-profits policies can be pretty complex, too, and many investors are not fully aware of the level of risk they may be taking with their money. Surprise, surprise, a large proportion of the mis-selling complaints that the financial ombudsman receives relate to with-profits funds.

Critics have accused firms of using the money from with-profits funds to benefit shareholders of the with-profits company itself rather than to protect policyholders' investments. And as the whole point of these funds is to keep money back (at least during the good years) in order to pay you later (you are told), it can be hard to know how much the company is pocketing and whether you're getting a fair deal.

What's more, if you decide you've been robbed and you want to get out you could find yourself charged for that. Exit penalties of up to 20% apply to many of these policies.

In short, if you've got money to invest, avoid with-profits funds.

> **What they want you to do:** invest as much as possible in with-profits products.
>
> **What you should do:** invest in a proper life-insurance policy if you need it then create a completely separate low-risk investment portfolio for yourself, if you are worried by the stock market, by spreading your investments across a range of asset classes, including some shares.

# Endowment Products

## WHAT THEY ARE

An endowment is basically an insurance policy, which pays out a lump sum at the end of a set period. Most endowment products are connected to mortgages. With an endowment mortgage, you don't repay any of the capital that you've borrowed. Your monthly payments only pay off the interest on the loan, plus the cost of life insurance (which ensures the loan will be paid off should you die). So, again, it's a mixed product with insurance and investment in the same bag.

The end goal of an endowment – and the big thing the 'advisers' used to use as an incentive to buy – is that by the end of the endowment period, your investments will have grown enough to enable you to pay off the original loan/mortgage 'and a little bit more'. That was the major carrot – the idea that you could pay it off and still have money left over for fun stuff.

Endowment mortgages were hugely popular during the 1980s when inflation and interest rates were high and you got tax relief on endowment premiums. Guess what, though – most of them didn't work.

## WHAT THEY ARE REALLY LIKE

Unfortunately, endowment products have a dismal rate of completion, with only a third reaching their full maturity date. Plenty (if not most) have been cashed in early, and many investors took out less than they put in.

The charges were the main reason why endowment products didn't work (I say didn't because there are hardly any on the market now). The estate agents and other 'advisers' were paid massive, up-front commissions to sell them then the fund managers took more than their pound of flesh out of your money before investing it. No surprise then, with the stock market not doing as well as predicted by the salespeople, the endowments did very, very badly for most people.

Endowment products are best avoided completely.

# Unit-Linked Products

### WHAT THEY ARE

A unit-linked policy is an investment-based life-insurance plan. The 'units' referred to are invested in different things then lumped together into one investment. Naturally, they're designed and run by fund managers who take their cut (a nice big one as there are lots of units and lots of things to do with these units) but you don't really get to see just how much of a cut.

The various units could be invested in the stock market, bonds, property or cash deposits. Different funds have different mixes of these assets and you can choose whether you go for a low-risk (low-return) one, a medium risk and return or high risk.

Essentially they take the principle of diversifying your money and do it all for you – for a price. Most of these types of funds also tend to carry large penalties if you need to cash them in early.

> **What they want you to do:** invest in these so that they can charge you huge fees every time they move.
>
> **What you should do:** set up your own diversified portfolio where you don't have to pay any management fees, just invest in a range of cheap products that work.

## Other Insurance Products to Be Wary Of

It's not just insurance-backed investments that are generally a bad idea – quite a few other insurance-based products should also normally be avoided. Things like:

PPI (payment protection insurance), which is designed to cover payments on a loan or an overdraft if the person who takes out insurance is unable to cover the repayments due to sickness or redundancy. It's a good idea in theory, but they tend to be packed full of escape clauses for the banks that sell them. (The elderly, the self-employed, people with existing medical conditions, those who didn't report all visits to the doctor, those who lost their job for any reason except compulsory redundancy and other groups are excluded from claiming.) What's more, even if you do successfully make a claim, the money in many cases does not cover their payments or last as long as they need.

In a few cases, PPI can be useful (if you are employed and you worry that if you are made redundant you couldn't repay the loan). If you think it would be useful to you then look on insurance comparison sites (including the insurance section of Moneymagpie.com) to find a well-priced policy. Don't take what your lender offers you – they aren't allowed to make you take out their insurance anymore but they will certainly try and sell it to you where possible.

MPPI (mortgage payment protection insurance) belongs to the same market as the above. When greedy banks get worried about unemployment levels rising, they often reduce their payouts while the premiums they charge for this type of cover rocket up.

However, again, MPPI has a place for many mortgagees. As with PPI, though, make sure you shop around for a good-value policy. Don't just take what your lender tries to sell to you. You can find better-priced insurance through comparison sites (including the insurance section on Moneymagpie.com) so shop around.

Unemployment insurance tends to come with a huge number of strings attached, and only 50% to 65% of your income is covered (up to a maximum benefit of £1,000–£2,000 a month for a year). On top of this, it can actually be very difficult to find a policy that just covers redundancy on its own. Most combine accident, sickness and unemployment in one pricey plan.

# Structured Products

## WHAT THEY ARE

Structured products are normally fixed-term products, typically lasting between three to six years, based on a selection of investments including scary things like derivatives, options, commodities and foreign currencies. Banks, financial advisers and dedicated structured product providers all sell them.

They are marketed (i.e. disguised) to appeal to cautious investors who want the benefits of investing in the stock market but without the risks (don't we all?). So they seem to offer greater rewards than a normal savings account, while keeping your capital just as safe. While this sounds great, it's not quite that simple – there are plenty of catches to be aware of.

## HOW DO THEY WORK?

Structured products can be boiled down to one of two main types: income or growth products.

### Income products
These plans promise a fixed income over a set period. The extra income is derived through investing a lump sum of your money. But the cash invested is not guaranteed – you only get your original money back if the stock market doesn't fall.

### Growth products
With growth products, no matter what happens in the stock market you will get your initial capital back (provided that the counter-party underwriting the claim doesn't default). But although your capital is normally guaranteed, growth isn't (despite the product's name!) Any growth is entirely reliant on the stock market, and there are no dividends to benefit from.

## RISKS OF STRUCTURED PRODUCTS

Though they're marketed as being a safe bet, structured products aren't quite as risk free as their sellers would like you to believe.

There are two main sets of risk to bear in mind: the risk that you might not get any benefits or growth from your investment, and the risk that you might lose some or even all of your original capital. Your basic capital could even be at risk in growth products if the counterparty (such as an investment bank) that is providing the capital protection goes bust. The same goes for any returns you may have been due – even if there was growth, if the relevant counterparty goes bust, you may not ever see that money.

Although those who sell structured products are regulated by the Financial Services Authority, the actual investments in these funds frequently aren't – which means you may not be covered by the Financial Services Authority compensation scheme.

## OTHER DISADVANTAGES

For something that's far from risk free, these products are not cheap. There are a whole host of charges – often buried from view in the fund's performance calculations – so you have no idea what you're really paying.

So once again if you pay for 'advice' or 'active management' of your investment then you can reckon on the costs for this 'help' being very high, the 'help' being anything but helpful and the returns going first into the fund manager's or bank's pockets long before it gets near you.

## WHAT'S THE ALTERNATIVE?

If you want to invest in the stock market, you could consider a simple tracker or ETF as I described in Chapter 4. It's a good long-term option, as they enable you to cash in your investment when the market conditions suit you. This is far better than putting your money in a structured product and being held hostage to fortune, praying that the market is in a good state by the time your structured fund has reached maturity.

# Venture Capital Trusts

## WHAT THEY ARE

Venture Capital Trusts (VCTs) are funds that invest in small start-up companies and businesses who are just emerging. VCTs are always looking for investors to provide them with capital, so that they in turn can invest in start-up companies that the VCT manager believes are a good bet.

These are unlisted businesses or shares that are listed on the Alternative Investment Market (AIM).

Different VCTs specialise in different areas. Some are gener-alist funds, investing in all sorts of different companies; some target management buy-outs; others concentrate on companies that operate in a particular sector.

Most VCT fund managers have a portfolio of companies they invest in, helping spread the risk and upping the chance of success to some extent. The aim is that many of the companies they invest in will grow and either be bought or floated on the stock market – bringing in healthy profits for the VCT and its investors.

## TAX ADVANTAGES

There are big tax breaks for those investing in VCTs as I mention in Chapter 8. You get a whopping 30% tax relief on small companies that have no stock-market quotation – plus you don't pay any tax on any profits or dividends. Even with these tax breaks, though, VCTs have performed very badly.

## ARE THEY WORTH IT?

Even if you're willing to take the risk, VCTs aren't cheap. There's often an initial charge of around 5%, while management fees are normally between 3% and 4%. Frequently there are also performance fees – so if certain targets are hit, these fees can all but wipe out the tax relief VCTs benefit from.

Compare that with the fees that are charged by standard trackers or exchange-traded funds (around 0.5%). Even actively managed funds only charge around 1.5%. There are potential rewards with VCTs, but exchange-traded funds overall are normally a far better bet.

# Enterprise Investment Scheme (EIS)

## WHAT THEY ARE

This is another tax break for people buying shares in unquoted companies. The scheme offers 20% tax relief and no tax on profits as long as you hold on to your shares for at least five years. This tax relief is available on investments of up to £500,000 a year in companies.

They are similar to VCTs – the main difference between the

two is that an EIS is an investment in a specific company, while a VCT invests in a number of 'risky' companies.

Even with the tax breaks, EIS investors have not done well and it seems like a lot of fuss over nothing to me!

## WHAT'S THE RISK?

The tax relief is this generous because EISs are so high risk. Not only that, but EISs are highly illiquid (i.e. difficult to sell and turn into cash), so it can be tricky to get your money out. There is no orthodox mechanism for individual investors to sell unquoted EIS shares, so it can be extremely difficult to offload them.

## ARE THEY WORTH IT?

Not unless you have a massive investment portfolio and can afford to gamble some of it without missing the loss or, as the companies marketing these put it, they are aimed at 'wealthier investors who can afford to take a long-term view and can accept falls in value'.

# Third Way Annuities

This is a classic case of 'if it looks too good to be true it probably is'.

Annuities as a whole are intended to offer the assurance of an income stream for life after you retire. The majority of people use their pension funds to buy annuities. However, most annuities are completely inflexible – they lock you into current interest rates. What's more, when you and your partner shuffle off this mortal coil, the payments stop (leaving nothing for any remaining family members).

Third way or 'variable' annuities, however, seem to provide a guaranteed lifetime income which is payable regardless of investment returns. Investment is 'locked in', in effect securing any gains.

This is the 'third way' – instead of choosing between:

a) an annuity that offers a protected income stream but has little growth potential, or
b) a full drawdown option that offers opportunity for investment growth, but no protection

Variable annuities aim to combine the best of both worlds.

So if the fund increases in value, the level of income will increase – but if the fund value drops, the income will remain the same. After your death, the funds can be paid as a lump sum to remaining family and loved ones.

On paper, this seems by far the best option. It's flexible, doesn't take unwarranted risks, will provide for both you and your partner as long as either of you are alive, and keeps its value in real terms . . .

Guess what – there are pitfalls. For starters, the guaranteed fixed income will initially be as much as 30% lower than a traditional annuity. Think about that for a moment – 30%, just under a third, lower.

Should the fund grow, this will rise, but that growth will depend on wider market conditions. And the fund requires much more management. Typical management fees come to between 0.5% and 1.5% a year, but they can total as much as 3% annually.

There is also the cost of the guarantee or insurance policy that assures the fixed income element of the plan. However, the economic crisis put underwriters on their guard and these guarantees are now much costlier. When you get massive volatility in the markets, the price of the guarantee increases significantly. Once the price gets too high, the product just doesn't work.

> **What they want you to do:** invest in these packaged-up, high-charging, complex products to make them money.
> **What you should do:** get more knowledge, be sceptical about anything that 'advisers' do a hard sell on and create your own portfolio.

So now you know what not to invest in – at least the generalities. Now, go back and look through some of the other chapters to remind yourself of what you should invest in, and how. Once you've done that, go back and take a look (at least a quick look!) at how to avoid tax while you're doing it. In the long run, cutting down the tax you pay is a very important aspect of making your investments work for you.

# Conclusion: The Future of Finance

Now, dear reader, you should have the tools in your hand to make your own informed decisions and beat the banks at their own game.

A few points I'm sure you have gleaned already that you should keep in mind:

- *If it sounds too good to be true, it probably is.*
- *No one product is 'safe as houses'. The safest way to invest is to 'diversify' – spread your money across various asset classes.*
- *Regard with mistrust any products that have the word 'guaranteed', 'high yield', 'with-profits' or 'bond' (apart from savings bonds, government bonds and corporate bonds) in them.*
- *Do your own research, think your own thoughts, invest according to your own calculations and ignore any hype and fear around you.*
- *In the world of finance, knowledge is power. Products are mis-sold mostly because of our ignorance. Keep adding to your*

*financial knowledge, bit by bit, here and there by reading financial articles on good websites (like Moneymagpie!) and broadsheet newspapers.*

- *Spending a few hours (or even days) researching specific investments may be boring but being poor in your old age is even more boring. Bite the bullet and go for it. You might even find (perish the thought) that some of what you read is actually interesting!*

- *Generally with investing, the simpler the product the better. Also, the lower the charges the better and the less they are packaged, mixed together or generally messed with by overpaid City boys the better.*

- *Any financial products advertised on billboards, in newspapers, on radio or (particularly) on daytime TV are likely to be pants. All these forms of advertising are expensive. Where do you think they get the money to pay for them? Their investors.*

So, with the information you've picked up in this book, what do you do now?

Firstly you get your finances sorted and start making a plan to invest regularly and well. Even if you've put no money away at all so far you can start now.

Secondly, decide that you are going to increase your knowledge and keep a good eye on your investments. You don't have to get obsessed with them – in fact, I urge you not to think about them too much. Go have a life. But every now and then do keep a wary eye on how they're doing.

Thirdly, get more involved in teaching your children, and others, how to invest and how to think about money.

Finally, get more involved in policy-making about finance,

financial education and the way our economy is run generally. Seriously – if you don't, who will? We've allowed the financial sector to get away with too much for too long. We have to insist that something is done.

# The Future of Finance

For too long our economy has been dependent very largely on the City. From the 1980s and the 'Big Bang', which allowed retail banks to get into stockbroking and all types of dodgy financial products, financial institutions have become fatter and more powerful by the week.

Even New Labour, when they came to power, adopted a hands-off approach to the men in pinstripe suits. This is because they had grasped the fact that the City was making such awe-inspiring profits that the tax revenue could support their social spending plan. We may hate bankers and rail at their inflated pay, grotesque bonuses and materialistic lifestyles but we also need to face the fact that our nation has lived off the fat of their profits.

This can't go on. This state of affairs where the City is allowed carte blanche to fleece us, the consumers, simply because the economy needs the tax money is unethical and (as we've seen in the recent crisis) unsustainable.

I run businesses and I know that if you rely on a single customer you're putting yourself in a very vulnerable position. Similarly, our economy cannot afford to rely so very much on the banking sector for its income. We need to revive manufacturing, improve small and large business in sectors other than finance and even support agriculture again. Who knows what will happen to the world economy this century, particularly with what seems to be unstoppable global warming. As the world's population grows we might find that food-producing land becomes the most valuable of all.

Whatever happens, though, the whole way that financial products are created and sold in this country has to change radically. New Labour brought in a few improvements such as stakeholder products that set a standard of transparency, fairness and low cost, but this is just a small start. Before them the Tories brought in PEPs and TESSAs (the forerunners of ISAs) which helped to encourage saving, but that was not enough either.

There are still far too many badly performing financial products that exist solely to take money straight out of our pockets and into those of the financial companies. There are far too many individuals dependent for their income on commissions they are paid when they sell horrible and useless financial products such as bad insurances, worse pensions and nasty rubbish thought up by the bank's R&D departments such as Payment Protection Insurance (PPI) and, recently, Identity Theft Insurance.

We must have fairer, clearer, simpler and more transparent financial products for consumers to use and invest in.

It has already been said (by Mervyn King among others) that banks need to have their activities split so that the day-to-day, utility side of the business (savings, current accounts, paying bills, etc.) is entirely separate from what the economist John Kay (Johnkay.com) calls 'the casino'. In other words, retail banking should be stopped from indulging in the mad, speculative, City-side of financial services. I agree.

Others say that this is not workable and that the two sides are far too closely entwined to be separated properly. But although I believe that the global investing side of finance has its place (and it's potentially a very lucrative one for the country), it's far too volatile to be so inter-connected with the needs of ordinary consumers. We need a whole new approach to consumer banking – one that is fair and profitable at the same time.

The word 'ethical' is bandied about a lot in our society – it's one of the many replacements for religion, I think – but it's the best word I can come up with for the way I consider banks should be run in the future. You don't have to be a tree-hugger to believe in paying a fair price for quality and good service. I consider that it is ethical to make a profit if you offer a good service, help people and make products that improve the common weal. Most Brits are quite happy to hear that John Lewis or Marks & Spencer have made a profit, even a fat one, as generally they feel that they get quality and service from both.

So that is what I mean when I say that banks need to be run on ethical principles. It's not just about producing brochures on recycled paper or bunging some cash at orphanages around the world every now and then to improve your brand image. It's deeper than that. It's about fundamental principles of business in which the customer is put first, service, honesty and efficiency are paramount and people are given genuine advice rather than sales talks.

Sounds impossible? I don't think so. If that were the way banks were run, particularly if (for the first time ever in their history) they were run efficiently using the latest technology (as opposed to being the last sector to embrace it every time), they would retain customers without effort, massively cut down on their advertising and marketing costs (and, now, legal costs) and make decent and honest profits. We need to follow the example of Credit Unions much more and get customers to be much more part of the running of their banks.

Crucially, though, the consumers – you and I – have to be educated. There is far too much ignorance of financial matters amongst the UK population and there are no signs of it improving any time soon. Truly, I believe that if we as consumers were thoroughly educated (or, frankly, even partially educated) in the way finances work and how to manage our money for short-term and long-term gain we would simply not allow the banks and other financial companies to get away with such bad practices. If you know something's junk and you know why it's junk, you're not going to buy it and the sellers of this junk will quickly dissolve and try to find something else that will work.

There will always be greed and fear and there will always be far too many people who are run by these destructive emotions too much of the time. However, if we had more knowledge of the principles of sensible and profitable money-management we would have far less mis-selling of financial products, a more even spread of wealth across the population and much less volatility in financial markets (including the property market).

Just as developing countries have totalitarian governments foisted on them because of widespread illiteracy (and, therefore, an inability to read information about their options for voting), so our financial illiteracy has allowed both companies and governments to pull the wool over our eyes and sell us bad products we don't understand . . . even after reading the literature!

If we are ever to haul ourselves out of third-world finance we have to get personal finance taught, and taught properly. I'm glad that it has now been set as an essential part of the curriculum and I only hope it will be taught properly. In my opinion we should also set up free adult education workshops around the country for the next 10 years in order to scoop up the millions (literally) of adults who have no more than a sketchy understanding of how to budget, save and invest for their futures.

I run money-management and investment workshops and seminars myself (find out about them at www.moneymagpie. com/workshops), but really the country needs a government-backed, nationwide initiative – as soon as possible.

## So What Should You Do Now?

YOU are in a much better position than the average consumer I have referred to above.

You have read this book (well, some of it – whichever bits were relevant) so you are already head-and-shoulders above most UK adults in terms of your financial knowledge. You have the tools now to run your own money and invest according to your own decisions, not other people's.

Here are the next steps I suggest you take:

- *Keep your knowledge topped up by subscribing to the newsletters of money and investment websites such as mine, Moneymagpie.com.*
- *Set an investment plan for yourself.*
- *Campaign for financial education for all, including adults. Join the 'Beat the Banks' campaign at www.moneymagpie.com/beatthebanks.*
- *Don't forget the day-to-day 'housekeeping' element of spending less than you earn, regularly (though not obsessively) checking*

*your money position and keeping abreast of money issues.*
- *If you want to learn more about investing, and about managing your money better, sign up for one of the Moneymagpie seminars. Just go to www.moneymagpie.com/workshops.*
- *Live a simpler life. Spend less, live more.*

**Investment is just a very small part of life, not the whole of it. Enjoy life!**

# Glossary

Accountant: Professional number-cruncher. Traditionally much maligned for having about as much charisma as a dial-tone, but come tax return time they can be your best friend, taking the headache out of your financial form-filling and saving you serious amounts of money.

Actuary: Someone who finds accountancy too racy.

Additional Voluntary Contribution (AVC): Extra payments you can choose to make into your pension, on top of what your employer asks you to pay.

Alternative Investment: Anything from gold, wine and Chippendale chairs to Ladybird books and Elvis memorabilia. Basically investments that are different from the traditional pensions, shares and property. They can also now include hedge funds and investment in small businesses.

Alternative Investment Market (AIM): The market for tiddlers. New and/or small companies that are not big and strong enough to be traded on the London Stock Exchange.

Annual Percentage Rate: A common way of expressing how much borrowing money will cost. It's the amount of interest you will be paying, over a year, on a sum you have borrowed.

Annual Equivalent Rate: The amount of interest your money will earn in a savings account if you leave it alone for a year.

Annuity: An income you're paid after you retire, until you die. You buy the annuity from a company, which then agrees to give you a fixed sum every year. Worth putting off pushing up the daisies for as long as possible or you'll lose out.

Blue Chips: Shares in the really big posh companies that are regularly at the top of the FTSE 100.

Bond: Nothing to do with James. More like an IOU: lenders hand over their money to a business or the government and expect to get it back, plus interest, in the future. There are many different kinds of bonds – they may be short term or long term and interest may be paid at a fixed or variable rate.

Capital: Ker-ching! A load of money! Or the value of your assets if you were to sell them.

Capital Gain: The profit you make when you sell an asset, e.g. the proceeds you get from selling shares, minus the cost of the shares. You have to pay capital gains tax on this profit if it goes above a certain threshold.

Capitalisation: The market price of an entire company, calculated by multiplying the number of shares outstanding by the price per share.

Compound Interest: see 'Interest'. Compound interest is a bigger version as it is calculated both on the sum and on the interest that has accrued on the sum in previous periods. Basically a get-rich-slow scheme.

Coupon: The slightly confusing interest-type payment that you are paid on a bond.

Defined Benefit Scheme: An occupational pension scheme with no surprises. Rules specify what you'll get when you retire, e.g. depending on what your salary is or how many years you've worked there.

Defined Contribution Scheme: An occupational pension scheme with surprises. Your contributions are fixed, but the amount of pension you finally receive will depend on things like the size of the fund that you've built up.

Derivatives: Financial products that are the counterpart of traditional securities. They 'derive' from the underlying asset. For example, a 'future' is an agreement to exchange the underlying asset (say some shares) at a future date.

Dividend: Money that companies give out to holders of stock (usually shareholders). British companies usually fork out a couple of dividends a year, one larger and one smaller. You usually get an amount for each share. The company decides how much of the profits (if any) share out and how much to reinvest in the business.

Dividend Yield: The share price divided by the annual dividend per share.

Dow Jones: A Welsh bloke who went to America to see some basketball matches. When he got there he found that basketball hadn't yet been invented. So while he waited he filled his time by making a list of all the companies whose shares you can buy on the New York Stock Exchange. It's still just as exciting as basketball.

EEA: see 'European Economic Area'.

Endowment: A combination of life-insurance policy and investment – you or your dependants are guaranteed a payout either on your death or on a fixed date, whichever is sooner. Generally expensive and poorly performing and a better money-maker for the person who sold it to you than for you.

Equities: A word for a plain old share in a company. Can also mean the amount of your house that you own (i.e. the value of the property minus any mortgage you still have to pay on it).

European Economic Area (EEA): A conglomeration of 30 countries established on 1 January 1994 which allows member states the free movement of goods, persons, services and capital. The 30 member states currently are Austria, Belgium, Bulgaria, Cyprus, Czech Republic, Denmark, Estonia, Finland, France, Germany, Greece, Hungary, Iceland, Ireland, Italy, Liechtenstein, Latvia, Lithuania, Luxembourg, Malta, Netherlands, Norway, Poland, Portugal, Romania, Slovakia, Slovenia, Spain, Sweden and the United Kingdom.

Exchange-Traded Funds (ETFs): A relatively new kind of investment fund which can be bought through most stockbrokers. They are similar to tracker funds as effectively they track the stock market. A cheap way to get into the stock market, as admin charges tend to be very low.

Final Salary Scheme: A rather nice little pension scheme, where you get an annual payout of a percentage of whatever your salary was when you retired. Expensive for employers to run, and consequently disappearing fast.

Financial Services Authority (FSA): Not to be confused with the similarly acronymed Food Standards Agency. The independent, non-governmental body that regulates the finance industry, including mortgages. In theory, the FSA should enforce good financial practice in the UK but so far has been a financial watchdog without much bite.

Front-End Loading: Nothing to do with washing machines, or any kind of domestic appliance for that matter. A front-end load is the initial admin and/or commission charge made when you invest in a unit trust, life-assurance company, or any other kind of investment fund.

FTSE ('Footsie'): The Financial Times Stock Exchange, i.e. the list of companies whose shares are available for public purchase on the London Stock Exchange.

FTSE All-Share Index: Includes around 700 of the top companies in the country.

FTSE 100 Index: A share index of the 100 biggest companies listed on the London Stock Exchange (LSE). The FTSE 250 tracks the big firms ranked at 101 to 350.

Friendly Society: Generally small, local bodies offering tax-efficient but mostly poorly performing financial products such as life policies and children's Investments.

Futures: The right to buy a particular share or commodity at a certain price on a future date.

Gearing (called 'Leveraging' in the US): Borrowing to invest in something (e.g. getting a mortgage to buy a house). The higher the percentage of your investment is from borrowed money the higher your 'gearing'.

Gilts: Bonds that are issued by the government.

Hedge Fund: An adventurous fund that attempts to make money even in (or particularly in) bad markets. Many use arbitrage as their main means of creating wealth. They can be volatile and usually charge sky-high fees. The minimum investment levels mean that most individual investors have no chance of putting money into them.

HM Revenue and Customs: Quite possibly the most exciting government department in the world. It has responsibility for all sorts of taxes, VAT, customs and excise, National Insurance, tax credits, child benefit and child trust funds, among other things. Find out more at hmrc.gov.uk.

Independent Financial Adviser (IFA): IFAs are licensed to advise you on financial products offered by a range of different companies. Some earn commission for selling particular products, which might lead you to question just how independent they really are. Truly independent advisers have access to the whole of the financial market and will charge you for their time.

Index Tracker: An index is, quite simply, a way of measuring how well a stock market is performing by comparing the performance of shares in a group of different companies. A tracker fund is basically a little baby microcosm of the index – shares in the same companies and in the same proportions they are found in the index. The idea is that the tracker will emulate the performance of the index, and hopefully get bigger as the market goes up.

Individual Savings Account (ISA): A way of saving money without having to pay tax on it. You can put up to £10,200 into ISA-wrapped investments each tax year. You can either put the whole lot into a shares ISA, or up to £5,100 into a cash ISA and the rest (up to £5,100) into a shares ISA.

Inflation: The tendency of prices to rise over time. This means the value of your money can drop if you don't keep up, e.g. by investing.

Inland Revenue: see 'HM Revenue and Customs'.

Intestate: Dying without having made a will.

Investment Trust: It's up to you whether or not you trust them. A company that invests its shareholders' funds in the shares of other companies. This might sound a bit Kafkaesque, but it means people without a lot of money can invest in a wide range of companies without incurring massive trading fees.

Leverage: see 'Gearing'.

Life Insurance: The term is often used interchangeably with life assurance, although technically, insurance protects holders from events that might happen. A type of policy where you pay a premium in order to get a lump sum paid out in the event of your death.

Managed Fund: A fund in which the fund manager charges you massive fees to make rotten investment decisions with your money (85% of the time anyway).

Mutual Society: A mutual is a company that has no issued stocks or shares. Instead, it is owned by its investors.

Negative Equity: A nasty little thing that can happen when house prices crash. If the value of your house falls below the value of your mortgage, you are said to have negative equity.

Nonsense: What most financial analysts talk. It often gets confused with 'accurate predications' because it is delivered with such confidence by men with posh voices

Occupational Pension Scheme: A pension scheme for employees of a particular company, or possibly a trade.

Open-Ended Investment Company (OEIC): A US idea that came over to the UK in 1997. A bit of a hybrid between a unit trust and an investment trust, OEICs sell shares in themselves then use that cash to invest in other companies. They usually operate as umbrella funds, often having a few different smaller funds. They're known as open-ended because, if demand for their shares rises, they simply issue more. Unlike in a unit trust, OEICs tend to just have one share price, whether you're buying or selling.

P/E Ratio: The ratio of the price of a share in a company to its earnings per share.

Personal Pension Plan (PPP): A pension scheme for those without occupational pensions, i.e. the self-employed and people whose employers don't have a group pension scheme. An employer can contribute to your PPP, but there's nothing to say they have to. You can take a PPP with you when you change jobs. PPP contributions get tax relief, and you can buy life assurance, which may also be eligible for tax relief. Apart from stakeholder pensions, though, PPPs tend to be expensive, opaque and badly performing.

Pound-Cost Averaging: The fact that by investing at regular intervals you buy when shares are low and when they are high. Over time these different prices average out to a medium price overall.

Rating Agencies: The much-maligned companies that provide risk ratings on governments, companies and bonds.

Retail Investor: You and me. Investors who are not professionals at it.

Risk: The key to all investments. The higher the risk the greater the chance of your losing your money and so the higher the return (often interest payment) that you will be offered. When people talk about 'pricing risk' this is what they mean.

Securities and Exchange Commission (SEC): The American financial watchdog. Like the FSA in the UK but much more proactive and political.

Security: A security is the precise opposite of what you think it would be. It's a piece of paper that says you own something: a share, a bond, a stock. It's a promise but how 'secure' the chances are of that promise being fulfilled depends upon the risk level with that particular share or bond.

Share: If you buy a share, then you own rights to part of the profits of a company and some other benefits. Roughly speaking, a company's share price is determined by market forces: if a lot of people want to buy shares, their value will go up, if a lot of people want to sell shares, their value will fall. So in theory, there's a lot of money to be made, but it's always a risk and if a company goes bust, shareholders are last in line to get any of the cash.

Shareholder: As the name suggests, anyone that holds shares in a company. Shareholders are also entitled to do stuff like receiving the company's accounts and voting at their Annual General Meeting. Most companies pay regular dividends to their shareholders.

Self-Invested Personal Pension (SIPP): A kind of DIY personal pension for people that know a bit about the stock market themselves. Rather than letting an insurance company decide where to invest your cash, you can choose what to invest in – including shares, property, art and antiques. Fees and charges for a SIPP usually work out at about 2% a year, though (they're capped at 1% in a stakeholder pension), so they're best reserved for those with lots of money to invest.

Stamp Duty: Another way the government punishes us for doing well. It's a fixed tax you pay when you buy shares (0.5%) or property above a certain price (1% to 4%, depending on the value of the property).

Stakeholder Pension: A fairly new type of low-cost, flexible pension. Even if you're not earning you can pay in a limited amount each year, and get tax relief on this. Anyone in a company pension scheme earning less than a certain amount a year (set by the HMRC) can pay into a stakeholder pension as well, and employers with five or more employees must give them access to a stakeholder scheme if the company doesn't have any other kind of pension fund set up.

Stock: The basis of many a good soup. What Americans call shares. And, in the UK, a fixed-interest financial asset like a government bond. There is usually a redemption date and, in the meantime, they are traded on stock exchanges.

Stock Exchange: A market on which securities are traded, such as the London Stock Exchange. The other big ones are in Tokyo and New York.

Stockbroker: An agent who does the trading on the stock exchange; usually far from broke. Now you can use much cheaper online brokers for buying and selling shares quite cheaply.

Tax: Money you have to pay to the government which, in theory at least, is then used to pay for useful things like the nation's health, education and politicians' lunches. There are many different kinds, e.g. income tax comes out of your pay packet and VAT which is charged on many goods that you buy (with the salary that has already been taxed). Basically, if you make a bit of money out of anything, the government wants a cut of it. Also known as 'daylight robbery'.

Tax Relief: A system whereby someone doesn't have to pay tax on part of their income. Always worth snapping up, if you qualify.

Total Return: The total amount you make on an investment, including both income and capital growth, as a percentage of the asset.

Tracker: A tracker is a shortened version of 'index tracker', something that automatically follows what is happening in the market – it 'tracks', for example, the FTSE 100 or the Oil and Gas sector.

Yield: The annual income you get from an investment, expressed as a percentage of the value of that investment. The interest rate on a savings account, for example.

## Appendix 1

# Summary

Here's a quick and easy guide to which products to invest in depending on your current needs and interests.

## Getting Started – Wondering What to Do First?

See Chapters 1 and 2 to get your priorities right, including, crucially:

- *Clear debts*
- *Create a cash buffer*
- *Start a stakeholder pension if you don't have access to a company one*
- *If you have dependants get a term life assurance policy*
- *Create a diversified investment portfolio according to your preferences for risk and return*

# Creating a Lucrative Investment Portfolio

The following recaps some of the different options available to you when creating your investment portfolio. I have not included investment options in this list that I don't like.

## BEGINNER

- *Savings accounts (page 70)*
- *Stakeholder pensions (page 140)*
- *Tracker funds (page 99)*
- *Gold coins (page 250)*

## INTERMEDIATE

- *Supermarket SIPP (page 144)*
- *Property (garages) (page 194)*
- *ETFs (page 104)*

## ADVANCED

- *Full SIPP (page 146)*
- *Property (page 198)*
- *Self-managed ISA (page 110)*
- *Stock-picking (shares, bonds) (page 113)*
- *Ethical funds (page 265)*

# Low-Risk Investments

- *Gilts (page 168)*
- *Gold coins (page 250)*
- *Savings accounts (page 70)*

# High-Risk Investments

- *Full SIPP (page 146)*
- *Property purchase and resale (page 198)*
- *Self-managed ISA (page 110)*
- *Stock-picking (page 113)*

# Long-Term Investments

- *Pensions (Chapter 5)*
- *Property rental/buy-to-let (page 205)*
- *Tracker funds (page 99)*
- *ETFs (page 104)*
- *Stock-picking (page 113)*
- *Corporate bonds (page 177)*
- *Ethical funds (page 265)*

# Medium-Term Investments

- *Property purchase and resale (page 198)*
- *Savings bonds (page 70)*
- *Gilts (page 168)*

# Short-Term Investments

- *Savings accounts (page 70)*

# Income-Bearing Investments

- *Annuities (page 148)*
- *Gilts (page 168)*

- *Investment-grade corporate bonds (page 177)*
- *Property rental (page 205)*
- *Savings bonds (page 70)*

# Investments with Growth Potential

- *Pensions (Chapter 5)*
- *Property purchase to upgrade (page 198)*
- *Shares, in all their forms (Chapter 4)*

# Low-Maintenance Investments

- *ETFs (page 104)*
- *Gold (page 248)*
- *Savings accounts (page 70)*
- *Stakeholders (page 140)*
- *Tracker funds (page 99)*

# High-Maintenance Investments

- *Full SIPP (page 146)*
- *Property rental (buy-to-let) (page 205)*
- *Self-managed ISA (page 110)*
- *Stock-picking (bonds or shares) (page 113)*

# How to Find a Good Independent Financial Adviser

Independent financial advisers (IFAs) come in all shapes, sizes and abilities, like accountants. It's important to see at least three or four before you plump for one:

- *Ask friends, colleagues and family for personal recommendations. Ask them why they like them (not just because they're a nice person!) Have these advisers genuinely saved or made them money?*
- *Get a free meeting with them. Most IFAs will give an initial consultation for free.*
- *First check that they are genuinely independent. If the answer is anything other than 'yes' (such as 'sort of' or 'partially') then, no matter how persuasive they sound about how that doesn't affect their ability to recommend great products, just walk out.*
- *Get them to give you contact details of other clients for references.*
- *Ask about fees. Do they charge fees on an hourly basis (good), do they earn their money from commission (not so good) or do they offer a mixture of the two (OK)? IFAs shouldn't charge fees as well as taking*

*commission. If you pay a fee, all the lump sum commission the IFA earns on financial products they sell you should be refunded to you.*

- *If you decide to go down the commission route, make sure you know how much your IFA will receive and that they genuinely can pick and choose products from the whole of the market.*
- *Ask them about their view of tracker funds. If they are not keen and just try to push managed funds on you then you should be wary. Also, see if they suggest tax-saving measures such as splitting your assets with your spouse. If they do not then they are not going to be good enough to advise you.*

For more information, including details of the qualifications your IFA must have, see Unbiased.co.uk (the website of IFA Promotion, the association for independent financial advisers). You can also find out more information on the Financial Services Authority (FSA) website at Moneymadeclear.fsa.gov.uk.

## BETTER STILL – CONSIDER A FINANCIAL PLANNER

While independent financial advisers have been trained to sell financial products, financial planners are much more geared towards looking at all aspects of your lifestyle, goals and needs, and developing a long-term financial strategy for you.

If you would like to have someone else taking a good long look at your life and your financial needs now and in the future, a planner would be better than an IFA.

To find a financial planner, the rules are the same as the ones for finding an IFA, although you can also go to the website of the Institute of Financial Planning in the UK which is at Financialplanning.org.uk.

# Useful Contacts

## Online Brokers

There are online brokers now including:

- TD Waterhouse: charge from £9.95 per online trade (www.tdwaterhouse.co.uk, 0845 6076002)

- Selftrade: charge £12.50 per trade – online, by telephone or via your mobile – and just £6 per trade when you qualify for its Frequent Trader scheme (www.selftrade.co.uk, 0845 0700720)

- Halifax Share Dealing: deal online for £11.95 (excluding international deals) or over the telephone from £15 (www.halifax.co.uk, 0845 7225525)

- Barclays Stockbrokers: standard online rate is charged at £12.95, but they also offer a rate of £9.95 when you make between 15 and 25 trades a month and £6.95 when you make 25 or more trades. Telephone commission is charged at a minimum of £17.50 (www.barclays.stockbrokers.co.uk, 0845 6017788)

- E*Trade UK: rates charged between £7 and £11.50 per trade, with reduced commissions for frequent traders (www.uk.etrade.com, 0845 2343434)

- Hargreaves Lansdown: deal online and over the phone from £9.95 per trade and begin trading the same day (www.h-l.co.uk, 0117 9009000)

- iDealing: deal online with rates charged from £8.91 (www.idealing.com, support@idealing.com)

- NatWest Stockbrokers: trade online at £15 per trade or over the phone at £35 per trade (www.natweststockbrokers.com, 0808 2084400)

- The Share Centre: trade online and over the phone from £2.50 per deal (www.share.com, 01296 414141)

# Tracker Funds

## MAJOR UK INDEX TRACKERS

**Fidelity Moneybuilder**
Index: FTSE All-Share
Annual charges: 0.10%
Minimum investments: £500 lump sum or £50 per month, top-up minimum £250
Website: www.fidelity.co.uk
Tel: 0800 414161

**Gartmore UK Index**
Index: FTSE All-Share
Annual charges: 0.5%
Minimum investments: £1,000 lump sum or £50 a month
Website: www.gartmore.co.uk
Tel: 0800 289336

**HSBC FTSE All-Share Fund**
Index: FTSE All-Share
Annual charges: 0.25%
Minimum investments: £1000 lump sum or £50 regular saver

Minimum additional: £500
Website: www.assetmanagement.hsbc.com/uk
Tel: 0800 289505

**iShares FTSE 100**
Index: FTSE 100
Annual charges: 0.4%
Minimum purchase: 1 share
Website: www.ishares.net
Tel: 0845 357 7000

**Legal & General UK Index**
Index: FTSE All-Share
Annual charges: 0.4%
Minimum investments: £500 lump sum, £50 monthly
Website: www.legalandgeneral.com
Tel: 0800 027 7169

**M&G Index Tracker**
Index: FTSE All-Share
Annual charges: 0.3%
Minimum investments: £500 lump sum, £10 monthly investment
Website: www.mandg.co.uk
Tel: 0800 390390

# Suggested Reading

*The Naked Trader*, Robbie Burns (Harriman House Publishing, 2007)
*The Essays of Warren Buffett*, LA Cunningham (John Wiley & Sons, 2009)
*Contrarian Investment Strategies*, David N Dreman (Simon & Schuster Ltd, 1999)
*Common Stocks and Uncommon Profits and Other Writings*, Philip A Fisher (John Wiley & Sons, 2003)
*The Intelligent Investor*, Benjamin Graham (HarperBusiness, 2005)
*The Long and the Short of It*, John Kay (The Erasmus Press Ltd, 2009)
*A Random Walk Down Wall Street*, BG Malkiel (WW Norton & Co, 2008)
*Daily Mail Tax Guide 2010/11*, Jane Vass (Profile Books, 2010)

# Recommended Websites

www.moneymagpie.com (of course!)

www.fool.co.uk

www.iii.co.uk

www.citiwire.co.uk

www.johnkay.com

www.freakonomics.com

# Index

# INDEX

*Also available from Vermilion by Jasmine Birtles*

# The Money Magpie

Packed full of practical financial advice and brilliant money-saving ideas, *The Money Magpie* shows you how to spend less, make more and invest what's left over, even in hard times. Based on this key idea, Jasmine Birtles tells you how to:

– get the best deals on utilities, credit cards and food
– assess and manage your finances with clear, easy-to-follow techniques
– make more money instantly using what you have already
– work out a long-term plan for increasing wealth that fits into your lifestyle

With handy links to Jasmine's fast-growing website www.moneymagpie.com, and the use of self-assessment quizzes, brilliantly simple advice and ideas that mould around the way you live, *The Money Magpie* will teach you how to be rich, whatever your situation.

£8.99                                    ISBN 9780091929466

**Order direct from www.rbooks.co.uk**